FILLED WITH THE HOLY SPIRIT

My Life Receiving, Exploring, and Experiencing Manifestations of God's Spirit

BY BOB CASHMORE

Library of Congress Cataloging-in-Publication Data available upon request.

Cover layout and design by Annalise Shadburne.

Editing by Mary Pero and Angie Emma.

Internal layout by Angie Emma.

ISBN: 979-8-9935528-0-4 (paperback)

ISBN: 979-8-9935528-1-1 (ePub)

Printed in the United States of America.

FILLED WITH
THE
HOLY
SPIRIT

*My Life Receiving, Exploring,
and Experiencing Manifestations
of God's Spirit*

BY BOB CASHMORE

In loving memory of
Larry and Audrey Eddings
whose faithfulness and teaching
led me deeper into life in the Spirit.

I am convinced and confident of this very thing, that He who has begun a good work in you will [continue to] perfect and complete it until the day of Christ Jesus [the time of His return].

Philippians 1:6, AMP

CONTENTS

Author's Note

The stories you are about to read are true. They come out of my own walk with Jesus and the experiences I've had with the Holy Spirit over the past forty years.

Because these stories often involve other people, I've chosen to change a name or two for the sake of privacy. What has not been changed is the truth of what happened, the power of God at work, or the lessons He taught me through them.

This book isn't meant to draw attention to me, but to point to the One who changed my life. My prayer is that as you read, you'll not only hear my story but also recognize the ways the Spirit is already moving in your own life—and be encouraged to open yourself more fully to Him.

— Bob Cashmore

INTRODUCTION

"Have you ever prayed the Sinner's Prayer?" a woman asked, gently touching my shoulder.

I'd been attending the Silverdale United Methodist Church for about a year, but I'd never heard of such a thing. I had no church background or real understanding of spiritual matters. I'd come forward during the altar call, overcome by shame and my own brokenness. I was desperate for Jesus to fix the mess I'd made of my life, but I didn't understand what that meant. *Giving your life to Jesus? The Sinner's Prayer?* What was that?

Two years earlier, I had this crazy idea that leaving England would magically erase the guilt I felt over my failed marriage. I thought that maybe I could just start all over again. But that dream quickly died after I arrived in Seattle, Washington with yet another disastrous relationship and a second divorce. Growing up in London during the war, my family only went to church on the rare occasion. I'd heard bits and pieces of the gospel as a teen in the Boys Brigade, but I didn't want it then. Now, I needed it.

Standing there at the altar, the woman invited me to repeat a simple prayer, and I gave my life to Jesus. I was already weeping, but suddenly my tears were a strange mixture of joy and gratitude. Something had changed. This was the second chance I'd been hoping for, but it hadn't come with changing countries, a new spouse or relationship, or even a new job. It had come from Jesus. "Therefore, if anyone is in Christ, he is a new creation. The old has passed away; behold, the new has come."[1]

It's been forty wonderful years since that Sunday when I went forward at the Silverdale United Methodist Church. But on that particular Sunday morning, I had no idea what I was doing. The idea that it might be a journey, or a process, had never occurred to me! I didn't realize I was entering into a *relationship* with Jesus, or that a few weeks later I'd be filled with the Holy Spirit—I'd never even heard of him!

In the book of Ephesians, Paul encourages us, "Don't be drunk with wine, because that will ruin your life. Instead, be filled with the Holy Spirit."[2] On the day of Pentecost, when the Holy Spirit fell on the church, some watching thought that the spirit-filled believers were just drunk. Peter corrected them, saying that the Holy Spirit had been poured out on them in accordance with the words of the prophet Joel.[3] It's a strange comparison, isn't it? You can be *filled* with the Holy Spirit, just like you can be *filled* with too much wine.

The thing is, I've met many Christians who don't seem to be filled with much of anything. They believe in Jesus, and they've heard of the Holy Spirit, but they don't have a *relationship* with the Holy Spirit. They've never experienced the manifestations of the Spirit. In an earlier trip to Ephesus, Paul met a group of believers much like the ones I'm describing. While Apollos was in Corinth, Paul traveled through the interior regions until he reached Ephesus, on the coast, where he found several believers.

"Did you receive the Holy Spirit when you believed?" he asked them.

"No," they replied, "we haven't even heard that there is a Holy Spirit."

"Then what baptism did you experience?" he asked.

And they replied, "The baptism of John."

Paul said, "John's baptism called for repentance from sin. But John himself told the people to believe in the one who would come later, meaning Jesus."

As soon as they heard this, they were baptized in the name of the Lord Jesus. Then when Paul laid his hands on them, the Holy Spirit came on them, and they spoke in other tongues and prophesied.[4]

Perhaps you've heard about the baptism of the Holy Spirit but haven't yet experienced a life *filled* with the Spirit. Maybe you've been taught that the Holy Spirit is only for charismatic churches. Or maybe you've come broken and hurting, desperate for the healing you've seen others receive. Jesus said, "I will ask the Father, and He will give you another Helper (Comforter, Advocate, Intercessor—Counselor, Strengthener, Standby), to be with you forever."[5]

The Comforter isn't just for the super-spiritual, the charismatic, or the disciples. He's for all of us.

This book is the story of what the Lord has done in my life; what happened in and through me after I was baptized in the Holy Spirit. It's the story of what it's like to have a relationship with Jesus, to be used by God, and to witness manifestations of the Holy Spirit. This isn't meant to be a theological study of who the Holy Spirit is, although I've included Scripture throughout for your reference. Instead, I hope you'll use this book as a guide to begin or deepen your own relationship with the Holy Spirit.

I've included my own experiences as illustrations and a guide to growing in and experiencing the different manifestations of the Spirit, but my experiences are not the final word on the matter. I'll also share what I consider to be important milestones, steps of growth, and manifestations of the Spirit I've seen. As with most things, you won't fully understand until you begin walking with and moving in the Spirit yourself. It's a lot like learning to swim—you won't learn just by listening to someone else talking about it. You need to get in the water and start flopping.

I've seen the Holy Spirit bring healing, wholeness, and purpose to both myself and others in ways I still struggle to explain. Things have happened that are beyond my understanding of what "normal" is, which is exactly what the Holy Spirit does: when we're willing, he takes the ordinary and the natural and does something supernatural. Something that only God can do. I'm excited to take you on this journey with me. Even though I had no idea what I was doing on that Sunday I first received the Lord, and was baptized in the Spirit a few weeks later, it really has been the best decision of my life.

CHAPTER 1

THE HELPER

I*t's probably a good idea to connect with other believers now that I'm a Christian.*

The idea had sounded reasonable enough when the pastor recommended it. And once I'd gotten over my nerves, I really enjoyed it. The small group was held in someone's home not far from where I lived. They welcomed me warmly, and the reading and discussion of God's Word had been lively. I felt the same sense of joy I'd felt a few days earlier. As the evening drew to a close, everyone gathered in a small circle and bowed their heads for prayer. One-by-one they each offered their prayers and petitions to God.

That's when I heard it.

A series of strange sounds slowly emerged from within the group. *What was going on?* I stole a quick glance around the prayer circle. A woman near me moved her mouth as if in prayer, but only a series of peculiar mutterings came out. It certainly wasn't English. Spooked, but with my head still bowed, I squinted around at the rest of the group. *What was happening?* I was extremely uncomfortable, but no explanation was made, and no one else seemed to mind.

The woman and her unusual "prayers" bothered me all week. *Was this part of what it meant to be a Christian? Was I missing something?* I wasn't sure. As I wrestled with my thoughts, I kept coming back to the one thing I did know to be true: I'd spent forty years trying and failing to do things my own way. Jesus had saved my life. If there was something more to walking with Jesus, I wanted to know about it.

BAPTIZED IN THE SPIRIT

"Last week during the prayer circle," I asked the following week at the small group. "The weird noises . . . could you please explain to me what that was all about?" I wanted some answers.

"Oh, that's nothing to be worried about," a woman named Gladys explained, "Pam was just praying in tongues, her spiritual language. That's between her and God."

My ignorance of spiritual things was so great that her answer meant very little to me. "Her spiritual language?" I asked. "Praying in tongues?"

"I have a book in my car about it," she said. "I'll go get it." Gladys returned a few minutes later with a book by Dennis Bennett. "Here," she said handing it to me. "Read this."

I'd been interested in spiritual things long before I became a Christian. I'd read some Russian mystics, but their answers hadn't satisfied my search for the true meaning of life. When I first moved to Seattle, a woman invited me to a Christian Scientology Center for inner healing. We talked for several hours—each of us holding tin cans connected by wires—stirring up painful childhood memories I thought I'd already dealt with. Something about the vibrations was supposed to be healing, but I was so emotional that when I later learned of the financial implications, I panicked and ran out of the building. I returned the next day to ask for my money back and for a reversal of whatever they started the day before.

But none of that prepared me for Dennis Bennett's book, *Nine O'clock in the Morning*. I finished it in record time. It's the story of

Pentecost—when the Holy Spirit was poured out on the church—and includes the author's testimony of being baptized in the Holy Spirit. I was fascinated, but now I had even more questions: *Was any of this real? Was it true? Was it in the Bible?*

Later that week, I walked to the church in search of the truth. I hoped one of the pastors would talk with me, but when I arrived, the church offices were empty. I hung around for a moment, somewhat defeated, when I heard a noise coming from the sanctuary. Inside I found Bud, a missionary to Liberia, who was home on furlough working at the church. He was familiar with the book and was open to talking with me about the Holy Spirit.

"Well," I said holding up the book, "is any of this real?"

Bud reached into his pocket and produced a small Bible. He flipped through the pages and began answering question after question from the Scriptures. I could hardly believe it. It was all true. It was in the Bible. More than that, the Holy Spirit was available to all who believed.

Just then, Don, a young man from my small group walked in. "I've been looking for you," he said. "Dennis Bennett's speaking at a Holy Spirit event in Bremerton tonight and I thought you might like to go." He'd been there when I asked about Pam praying in tongues, but why he'd come to look for me at the church, I had no idea.

"Yes!" I said, somewhat surprised by the turn of events. How strange that I was holding Dennis Bennett's book in my hand, asking Bud questions about the Holy Spirit, and being invited by Don to a Dennis Bennett event about the Holy Spirit later that night!

"What time is the meeting? And where exactly is it?"

"I'm not sure," Don said, "but why don't I pick you up at 6:30 p.m. tonight and we'll drive around Bremerton until we find a crowded church parking lot."

THE HOLY SPIRIT

Before reading Dennis Bennett's book, I had never heard of the Holy Spirit, let alone the baptism of the Holy Spirit. But the book of Acts describes Pentecost—the day the Holy Spirit was given to the church— in great detail. It happened! In fact, many churches still celebrate Pentecost as part of the liturgical calendar. I'm sure the whole thing seemed weird and strange to the early believers as well, but it was real!

> When the day of Pentecost came, they were all together in one place. Suddenly a sound like the blowing of a violent wind came from heaven and filled the whole house where they were sitting. They saw what seemed to be tongues of fire that separated and came to rest on each of them. All of them were filled with the Holy Spirit and began to speak in other tongues as the Spirit enabled them.[1]

Soon, a crowd gathered, amazed by the sight and the sound—each one could hear the believers speaking in their own language! The situation was so strange that many onlookers thought the believers were drunk. Then Peter got up to preach:

> Fellow Jews and all of you who live in Jerusalem, let me explain this to you; listen carefully to what I say. These people are not drunk, as you suppose. It's only nine in the morning!
> No, this is what was spoken by the prophet Joel: "In the last days, God says, I will pour out my Spirit on all people. Your sons and daughters will prophesy, your young men will see visions, your old men will dream dreams. Even on my servants, both men and women, I will pour out my Spirit in those days, and they will prophesy."[2]

Before he died, Jesus promised his disciples that he would send them a Helper, the Holy Spirit. In fact, in John 16:7, he told his disciples it was to their *advantage* that he go away, because if he didn't, the Helper would not come. He instructed them to wait for the promised Holy Spirit, saying that when the Spirit came upon them, they would receive power, and the Spirit would guide them into all truth.[3] So while the disciples had *heard* about the Holy Spirit before the day of Pentecost, on that day—when the Spirit was poured out upon them—they had a new *relationship* with him.

When I went forward for prayer that Sunday, I needed Jesus right then. In that moment. I didn't understand that the Christian walk is a progression. We have faith to believe and receive salvation, but it doesn't end there. That's only the beginning. I had no idea who the Holy Spirit was, but I was about to find out. My relationship with the Holy Spirit was about to change.

THE THIRD PERSON OF THE TRINITY

The Holy Spirit is God, the third person of the trinity. He is not an "it" or a "thing." He is found in both the Old and New Testaments, beginning with the opening lines of Genesis. "In the beginning, God created the heavens and the earth. The earth was without form and void, and darkness was over the face of the deep. And the Spirit of God was hovering over the face of the waters."[4]

Jesus commanded his followers to baptize new believers in the name of the Father and of the Son and *of the Holy Spirit*.[5] And in the book of 2 Corinthians, Paul prayed, "May the grace of the Lord Jesus Christ, the love of God, and the fellowship of the Holy Spirit be with you all."[6] In Romans, we learn that the "Spirit of God" who raised Jesus from the dead also lives in us.[7] This is a foundational truth of our faith.

So why is the Holy Spirit essential in some churches and left out of others? If the Holy Spirit was instrumental in raising Jesus from the dead and an important part of our theology, why don't we hear more about him on Sunday mornings? I would argue the Holy Spirit is often left out, misrepresented, and abused because we don't understand him. God as the Father is a relationship we can grasp. Jesus as the Son, Friend, and Brother we can appreciate. But the Holy Spirit or Holy Ghost, as he used to be called, well . . . that's a bit harder to wrap our heads around.

To further complicate the matter, Scripture teaches that the Spirit works and lives within us—in an unseen spiritual world—making his movements and works more difficult to talk about. Here's the problem: if we haven't been taught about the Holy Spirit, how do we know we need him? If he's only some "ethereal spirit" who touches people once in a while, why would we call on him for help at all?

I've met too many Christians who have never met the Holy Spirit. They've heard of him. But they haven't been baptized in the power of the Holy Spirit. They are trying to live the Christian life in their own power, which never works. They are frustrated, confused, and hurt. Trying to walk through life in your own power was never what God had in mind. Paul tells us in the book of Ephesians that the Spirit gives us inner strength so that Christ can make his home in our hearts.

> I pray that out of his glorious riches he may strengthen you with power through his Spirit in your inner being, so that Christ may dwell in your hearts through faith. And I pray that you, being rooted and established in love, may have power, together with all the Lord's holy people, to grasp how wide and long and high and deep is the love of Christ, and to know this love that surpasses knowledge—that you may be filled to the measure of all the fullness of God.[8]

We need to be born in the Spirit, that is, born a second time in the spiritual realm, filled with the Holy Spirit, and walk in the Spirit to experience the abundant life that Jesus promised. The Spirit doesn't just make our lives better—he makes them possible, and infinitely richer and more wonderful than we can possibly fathom.

DO YOU WANT TO RECEIVE HIM?

Later that evening, Don and I drove around Bremerton until we found a full parking lot at Saint Paul's Episcopal Church. We made our way inside and found our seats. After reading Dennis' book, I was very eager to hear him speak. Dressed in a light gray suit with a purple shirt and white collar, Dennis Bennett looked to me like the quintessential

English vicar—minus the black cassock. He had silver hair and spoke with a soft English accent. After a wonderful teaching on the Holy Spirit, he asked if anyone was interested in receiving the Holy Spirit.

My hand shot up.

I tried to pull it down. I don't even remember making the decision to raise my hand, but it stayed raised until I was invited into a small room with perhaps a dozen other people who also wanted to receive the Holy Spirit.

After a few minutes, Dennis joined our group and gave a beautiful cleansing prayer, asking for God's forgiveness over our lives and inviting the Holy Spirit to purify our hearts, as well as the room, from any demonic presence or influence. It felt incredible to be washed by a prayer, which, aside from the Sunday morning when I received Christ, I'd never really experienced before.

Dennis then began to move around the room, spending a few minutes speaking privately with each person there. A few others had now joined us, in addition to those wanting to be baptized in the Spirit. They walked around the edge of the room, praying and speaking in tongues all at once, a cacophony of unintelligible sound and energy filling the room.

Something was happening just like at the small group, but I had no idea what. This looked and sounded like what Dennis had spoken of earlier, what I'd read about in his book, and what Bud had showed me in the Bible, but experiencing it—this other-worldly, supernatural occurrence—felt uncomfortable, frightening even.

"Do you want to receive the baptism of the Holy Spirit?" Dennis asked. He stood in front of me, patiently waiting while I just stood there. It was my turn, but I couldn't say anything.

"You know," Dennis said, "Satan does not want you to ask for the gift of Jesus' baptism with the Holy Spirit. He's probably telling you right now not to believe it."

That was *exactly* what I had been thinking.

"That's spiritual warfare," Dennis said, his soft English accent both calming and reassuring me. He shared a few more things about spiritual warfare before asking me again if I wanted the baptism of the Holy Spirit.

"Yes," I finally said. "I want it."

Dennis placed his hands on my head, while others gathered around laying their hands on my shoulders, arms, and back. As he prayed, I suddenly felt the release of the Spirit well up inside me. It was like a fountain overflowing. I began to weep tears of joy and found myself laughing with relief and thankfulness for what God had done. I had been so afraid, and yet, this was wonderful. I had received the fullness of God's Spirit.

REFLECTION & PRAYER

I became a new creation and began my new life as a Christian in April of 1984, the Sunday I went forward for prayer and received Jesus my Lord and Savior. I had a clear before and after. A few weeks later, I was baptized with the Spirit. My life has never been the same. As I talk with believers about the baptism of the Holy Spirit, I like to first ask them their testimony. Talking with Nicodemus, Jesus told him, *You must be born again*.

Have you been born again?

For those of you raised in a Christian home, I don't just mean when you believed in Jesus. Even the demons believe. When did you confess that you are a sinner and in need of the saving grace that Jesus offers to each one of us? If you aren't sure, I encourage you to make that confession and commitment to him as your Lord and Savior right now! If you know your testimony but aren't sure if or when you've received the baptism of the Holy Spirit, let's ask God for that together.

We often see the baptism of the Holy Spirit coming with the laying on of hands. In Acts 8, we see the Spirit given to the Samaritans when the disciples laid their hands on them.[9] Later, we see that spiritual gifts were given to Timothy through prophecy with the laying on of hands.[10] In the book of Hebrews, we learn that the laying on of hands was a foundational doctrine of the faith.[11] That is certainly what happened in my own life, just as it happened on Pentecost, when the disciples "laid their hands on them and they received the Holy Spirit."[12]

If you want to be baptized in the Spirit, I recommend you meet with the elders and other believers at your church. Let them know of your desire to be baptized in the Spirit and ask them to pray for you with the laying on of hands. Being in community with other believers is essential to our Christian walk.

Most of us have heard the Scripture where Jesus instructs us to ask, seek, and knock. But in context, Jesus is encouraging us to *ask for the Holy Spirit*:

> So I say to you: Ask and it will be given to you; seek and you will find; knock and the door will be opened to you. For everyone who asks receives; the one who seeks finds; and to the one who knocks, the door will be opened.
>
> Which of you fathers, if your son asks for a fish, will give him a snake instead? Or if he asks for an egg, will give him a scorpion? If you then, though you are evil, know how to give good gifts to your children, how much more will your Father in heaven give the Holy Spirit to those who ask him![13]

In the next chapter, I'll share more about what happened on the night I was baptized with the Holy Spirit. For now, I'll leave you with these closing thoughts and questions for your reflection and prayer.

- What is your testimony of salvation? What is your before and after?
- Have you been baptized with the Holy Spirit?
- Do you want to receive the baptism of the Holy Spirit?
- Ask God to prepare your heart to receive the Holy Spirit. Share your desire with trusted believers at your church or small group. Ask them to lay hands on you and pray for the baptism of the Holy Spirit.

Chapter 2

Learning to Speak

The steady hum of people speaking in tongues reverberated all around me. My friend Don hadn't stopped praying in tongues since he joined us in the room earlier—a series of weird noises that occasionally surged with what sounded like excitement and urgency. I'd felt joy and relief only moments earlier, but those feelings had quickly turned to dread. The expectation, of course, was that I would begin to speak in tongues.

But I wasn't going to let that happen.

Dennis still stood in front of me with one hand on my shoulder as Don continued his endless stream of chattering sounds. Dread became agitation, and I suddenly felt irritated by all these people praying in tongues and (it seemed to me) pressuring me to do the same. *Nothing's coming out of my mouth that I can't understand!*

I was irritated by Don praying right behind me. *How rude.* I was irritated with Dennis and his patient expectation—his refusal to walk away and accept that I was not going to speak in tongues. And I was irritated with myself for feeling pressured in the first place.

"Just open your mouth and allow the sound to come out," Dennis said softly. "Even if it doesn't make sense to you . . . let it out."

This is silly.

"It's like a baby making their first sounds as they learn to talk," Dennis continued.

I could feel myself softening to the possibility. I opened my mouth just a bit, when suddenly, a few little clicking sounds came out.

"Go on . . ." he said.

And I did.

EVIDENCE OF THE SPIRIT

When the Holy Spirit was given to the church on the day of Pentecost, the believers began speaking in tongues, or languages unknown to them.

> Now there were staying in Jerusalem God-fearing Jews from every nation under heaven. When they heard this sound, a crowd came together in bewilderment, because each one heard their own language being spoken. Utterly amazed, they asked: "Aren't all these who are speaking Galileans? Then how is it that each of us hears them in our native language?[1]

But this isn't the only time we see evidence of the Holy Spirit working through the manifestation of tongues. As the church began to grow, Peter visited a God-fearing gentile and centurion named Cornelius after receiving a vision from God. Peter shared the gospel with them, and while he was still speaking, the Bible says, "the Holy Spirit came on all who heard the message." The evidence that the Spirit had come? "They heard them speaking in tongues and praising God."[2]

On one of Paul's missionary journeys in Ephesus, he came across a group of believers who had not yet received the Holy Spirit. They'd never heard of him. They only knew part of the story—John's baptism.

> Paul said, "John's baptism was a baptism of repentance. He told the people to believe in the one coming after him, that is, in Jesus." On hearing this, they were baptized in the name of the

Lord Jesus. When Paul placed his hands on them, the Holy Spirit came on them, and they spoke in tongues and prophesied.[3]

John the Baptist preached a message of repentance in preparation for the kingdom of heaven—the coming of Jesus.[4] But Jesus never contradicted John's message or baptism. In fact, speaking to the crowds about John, he told them that John was a prophet, yes, but also more than a prophet. "[John] is the one about whom it is written: 'I will send my messenger ahead of you, who will prepare your way before you.'"[5] John's baptism of water and repentance pointed people to Jesus.

I bring this up because I believe many Christians today have only heard part of the story. They've heard about and received salvation through Jesus, but they've never received the baptism of the Holy Spirit that Jesus pointed to. In his last days with his disciples, Jesus told them about the coming Holy Spirit. Jesus wasn't pointing the way to someone else, like John. Just before he promised the Holy Spirit, he told them, "I am the way, and the truth, and the life."[6] He was pointing the way to himself through a relationship with the Holy Spirit.

And I will ask the Father, and he will give you another advocate to help you and be with you forever—the Spirit of truth. The world cannot accept him, because it neither sees him nor knows him. But you know him, for he lives with you and will be in you. I will not leave you as orphans; I will come to you.[7]

Jesus didn't say, *Memorize what I said and did and you'll be fine*, or *Keep memorizing Scripture and go to church—I'll see you there*. Those are good things, but like John's baptism of repentance, they will only get you so far. Jesus didn't leave us alone, as fatherless orphans. He gave us the Holy Spirit.

ALIVE IN THE SPIRIT

During their late-night conversation, Jesus told Nicodemus, "Truly, truly, I say to you, unless one is born again he cannot see the kingdom of God."[8] But that confused Nicodemus. Jesus answered a question Nicodemus hadn't asked with a riddle. *Born again? How is that possible?* Jesus explained, "Very truly I tell you, no one can enter the kingdom of God unless they are born of water and the Spirit. Flesh gives birth to flesh, but the Spirit gives birth to spirit."[9]

Jesus is describing two very different lives. The first birth is physical and experienced on the day we come into the world. But the second birth, Jesus says, is of the Spirit. It is a new spiritual life in the kingdom of God, accessed through a personal relationship with Jesus Christ. In the book of Romans, Paul described these two births from the perspective of our spiritual inheritance. Through Adam, sin entered the world, and death through sin. But in Jesus, we receive life.

> Therefore, just as sin entered the world through one man, and death through sin, and in this way death came to all people, because all sinned—
>
> ... if the many died by the trespass of the one man, how much more did God's grace and the gift that came by the grace of the one man, Jesus Christ, overflow to the many![10]

We begin our spiritual lives in much the same way that we begin our lives in the physical world—as babies. We *learn* how to speak and how to walk. And we definitely don't get it right all the time. We stumble and fall, don't we! Peter, talking about this spiritual progression said, "like newborn babies, crave pure spiritual milk, so that by it you may grow up in your salvation."[11] Paul puts it a little more bluntly, "When I was a child, I talked like a child, I thought like a child, I reasoned like a child. When I became a man, I put the ways of childhood behind me."[12]

Most parents remember the baby stage with fondness, but we still expect our kids to grow up. It would be weird if we stayed spiritual babies forever. But such is the case for so many believers. We believe in the Holy Spirit, but we are afraid of spiritual things we don't understand. We never develop. We haven't yet grown into spiritual maturity.

Paul faced this very issue with the Corinthians, "I could not address you as people who live by the Spirit but as people who are still worldly— mere infants in Christ. I gave you milk, not solid food, for you were not yet ready for it. Indeed, you are still not ready."[13] The author of Hebrews says much of the same, "though by this time you ought to be teachers, you need someone to teach you the elementary truths of God's Word all over again. You need milk, not solid food."

PRAYING IN THE SPIRIT

It would seem that speaking in tongues, or praying in the Spirit, is part of how we grow into spiritual maturity. In his letter to the church, Jude, the half-brother of Jesus, encouraged us keep ourselves in God's love "by building [ourselves] up in [our] most holy faith and praying in the Holy Spirit."[14] In the book of Ephesians, Paul added, "And pray in the Spirit on all occasions with all kinds of prayers and requests."[15] Praying in Spirit is our prayer language. Like Pam praying in tongues during our prayer circle, it's a way for us to speak to the Spirit about spiritual things, spirit to spirit. It's a way to build up our faith and grow into spiritual maturity.

But we don't always know what to pray for or how to pray, do we? Many of us have never prayed aloud in a group setting, let alone used our prayer language in the Spirit. Like children, we must learn. Romans tells us that when we don't know what to pray for or how to pray, the Holy Spirit prays for us with groanings too deep for words. Praying in tongues frees us from restraints of language when we don't know how to pray, or when what we're praying for is more than we can find words to express. Paul said he did both.

I will pray with my spirit, but I will also pray with my understanding; I will sing with my spirit, but I will also sing with my understanding. Otherwise when you are praising God in the Spirit, how can someone else, who is now put in the position of an inquirer, say "Amen" to your thanksgiving, since they do not know what you are saying? You are giving thanks well enough, but no one else is edified.[16]

We pray in tongues, and we also pray in the language both we and others can understand. One is not necessarily separate from the other. You might be praying in tongues and then pray something with your understanding. It may be the same thing that you're praying in tongues, but you don't know. It's okay to do both.

WHAT ARE YOU AFRAID OF?

After the first few clicking noises, I made even more sounds. I just let it out, and as I did, I felt something like happiness bubbling up inside of me. I'm still not sure how to describe the feeling all these years later. It was a wonderful feeling of joy welling up inside. I had no idea what I was saying, whether it was a known language to someone else, or the language of angels as I've heard some people say. I just know that it was wonderful.

"Keep on talking to God," Dennis said quietly, "this is your private prayer language." And then he walked off to the next person as I stood there speaking in tongues—the very thing I had been so afraid of—and praising God. My life has never been the same. I had a peculiar sense of triumph—as if all of my past failures in life had been defeated. I had been baptized with the Holy Spirit and empowered to be a witness and give glory to God. Soon I would be making a public declaration of my faith in Jesus through the sacrament of water baptism.

There is inevitably a struggle when we talk about speaking in tongues. I was resistant because I didn't understand it. I was afraid. My past experiences had made me wary of my own emotions—I didn't trust them. I had tried to shut them off (along with Jesus) a long time ago. There might be something holding you back or limiting you spiritually.

When we are born again, we receive spiritual healing through faith in Christ; Adam's sin is done away with. But nevertheless, the sin nature in our minds, our will, and our emotions still wants to rule and reign over us. That's the battle of the flesh that Paul talks about. "I do not understand what I do. For what I want to do I do not do, but what I hate I do."[17] We're saved. We're born again. But we're still stuck in past sins, memories, or wounds we thought we'd already dealt with.

If speaking in tongues is a way to build up your faith and connect more deeply to the Father—then Satan doesn't want you to have it. When Dennis prayed for me, I experienced what spiritual warfare was like for the first time. The deceiver was actively trying to prevent me from receiving what Christ had for me. Satan doesn't want you to speak in tongues, but why wouldn't *you* want it? What are you afraid of? Without the Spirit's activation and freedom in your life, you'll struggle to overcome sin, live abundantly, and experience the function of the other gifts in your life.

REFLECTION & PRAYER

In John 4, there's a beautiful story about acceptance, forgiveness, and the healing love of God. You're probably familiar with the story, but let me tell you why it's so powerful to me. First, let's read about Jesus' stop in the town of Samaria:

> Now he had to go through Samaria. So he came to a town in Samaria called Sychar, near the plot of ground Jacob had given to his son Joseph. Jacob's well was there, and Jesus, tired as he was from the journey, sat down by the well. It was about noon.
>
> When a Samaritan woman came to draw water, Jesus said to her, "Will you give me a drink?" (His disciples had gone into the town to buy food.)
>
> The Samaritan woman said to him, "You are a Jew and I am a Samaritan woman. How can you ask me for a drink?" (For Jews do not associate with Samaritans.)[18]

Jesus' request broke tradition with all the known protocols at the time. Men wouldn't speak to a woman they didn't know in public, and Jesus, a Jew, certainly wouldn't be speaking to a Samaritan. But he did. In fact, the first sentence tells us that he *had* to go through Samaria, when most Jews walked the long way around. Jesus wasn't bothered by what society said about the woman or where she lived. He wasn't put off.

> Jesus answered her, "If you knew the gift of God and who it is that asks you for a drink, you would have asked him and he would have given you living water."
>
> "Sir," the woman said, "you have nothing to draw with and the well is deep. Where can you get this living water? Are you greater than our father Jacob, who gave us the well and drank from it himself, as did also his sons and his livestock?"
>
> Jesus answered, "Everyone who drinks this water will be thirsty again, but whoever drinks the water I give them will never thirst. Indeed, the water I give them will become in them a spring of water welling up to eternal life."[19]

Suddenly, Jesus changed the conversation to spiritual things—living water—and we learn that she had not only been married five times, but the man she was with now wasn't her husband. Still, there was no condemnation. He knew everything about her: her shameful past, her hiding, and her wounds. But he did not condemn her.

The woman—fully known, seen, and loved—was so blown away that she ran into town to tell everyone she knew about Jesus. She was healed that day. Something inside of her broke open when she received God's unconditional love. That was my story too. Maybe you need to be reminded of God's deep love for you. Like the Samaritan woman did. Like I did. Jesus knows the truth about us, but he's still loving enough to give us grace. He loves you so much that he sent his only Son, Jesus, to die for you while you were still a sinner. The Bible teaches that nothing—not even death—can separate us from his great love.

Open your mouth and let it all out.

- Pray and ask the Holy Spirit to reveal any unforgiveness or brokenness that may be holding you back. Ask him, "Holy Spirit, why am I afraid to trust you? Why am I afraid to put my faith in you? What's holding me back from going deeper with you?"
- If the Holy Spirit reveals something to you, offer it back to him in the form of prayer, groanings, or tears. It doesn't matter. Remember, the Holy Spirit is interceding for you. Talk to him about it.
- Find a place where you feel safe to explore your spiritual language and talk to God. Think about how God has forgiven you, washed you clean from your sins, and given you a new song of praise to sing to him. Open your mouth and let it out.
- If you're just beginning your new spiritual life, or taking baby steps, I recommend praying to the Holy Spirit. He is God—there's nothing wrong with talking to him. It will help you understand him as a person and become better acquainted with him as your Helper and Advocate.

CHAPTER 3

LEARNING TO LISTEN

I *'ve got to go see Connie.* I was giddy with excitement. *I need to tell her what happened!*

As soon as Don dropped me off after the event, I raced over to Connie's house. She and I had been dating for about a year at that point and were spending more and more time together. We'd both experienced similar difficulties with previous failed relationships, and we wanted to do things differently this time. We'd taken our kids on trips together. We were hopeful of a lasting future together and had even begun to talk about marriage. It wasn't easy to talk with her about my hopes and regrets, but I did. Gradually, she trusted me with hers too. She had to know the good news.

I knocked on her door.

"Hey, Connie, guess what?" I blurted out the moment she opened the door. "I just got baptized with the Holy Spirit!"

She stared at me blankly for a moment before shaking her head. "That's it! I'm not marrying a holy roller!"

I was dumbfounded. I expected her to rejoice with me. This was good news! Connie and I had been going to church together, but for her, this was one step too far. I worried this might really be it for us, but

God's grace prevailed because Connie—although not impressed—was willing to listen. She tried to understand, but she didn't buy it. The more I continued to share however, she realized that similar things had taken place in her walk with the Lord. The baptism of the Holy Spirit wasn't so far out there as she initially feared.

I drove home that night feeling somewhat better about our situation, even if I was a bit disappointed that Connie didn't share my excitement. Receiving the Holy Spirit had been a very significant moment in my life. Of course, this was where the real test began. I had been baptized in the Spirit, but now my old ways of thinking and living needed to be changed. I needed to learn from the Holy Spirit how to walk in this new life and—I hoped—build a lasting relationship with Connie. I needed the Holy Spirit to speak to me, and I needed him to speak to her as well!

Speak Lord, Your Servant Is Listening

Throughout the book of Acts, we see the Holy Spirit speaking to his people. As the believers of the early church in Antioch gathered together, the Scriptures tell us, "While they were worshiping the Lord and fasting, the Holy Spirit said, 'Set apart for me Barnabas and Saul for the work to which I have called them.'"[1] The Holy Spirit didn't just give an impression—he spoke audibly. They all heard him! A few chapters later however, Paul tells us he "felt compelled by the Spirit," to go to Jerusalem even while the Holy Spirit warned him that he would face prison and many hardships there![2] What does that mean? We don't really know, only that it was the Spirit speaking to him.

In the Old Testament, we read the story of the first time the Lord spoke to Samuel the prophet when he was only twelve years old. Young Samuel had been serving and living in the house of the Lord with Eli the priest ever since his mother, Hannah, dedicated his life to the Lord. Then one night, as he lay down to sleep, the Lord called him. Samuel answered, "Here I am." And ran to Eli's room saying again, "Here I am; you called me."

But Eli hadn't called Samuel. Tired and unbothered, Eli sent Samuel back to his room. "I didn't call you. Go back to bed."

So, Samuel went back to his bed and lay down. Then the Lord called Samuel a second time. "Samuel!" the Lord called.

Just as before, Samuel got up and went into Eli's room, "Here I am; you called me." But Eli hadn't called him, and so again, he sent Samuel back to bed. And here, in the middle of the story, we see the key verse: "Now Samuel did not yet know the LORD: The word of the LORD had not yet been revealed to him."[3]

Imagine hearing the voice of God and not knowing it was him! But I think this happens to Christians all the time. We're so caught up in debating whether the Spirit still speaks, whether he speaks audibly or through feelings. We're missing the point! God was speaking to Samuel, but Samuel didn't yet know the Lord—*he didn't recognize the Spirit's voice.*

The third time Samuel came running into Eli's room, Eli realized it was the Lord. So this time, he sent Samuel back to his room with some instructions:

"Go and lie down, and if he calls you, say, 'Speak, LORD, for your servant is listening.'" So Samuel went and lay down in his place.

The LORD came and stood there, calling as at the other times, "Samuel! Samuel!"

Then Samuel said, "Speak, for your servant is listening."[4]

THE GENTLE WHISPER

The Holy Spirit wants to speak to you. He may already be speaking to you, and like Samuel, you haven't yet recognized his voice. Did it sound like a thought? An audible voice? A feeling? In each of the previous examples, how the Spirit communicated was different. Samuel heard the Spirit call, but Eli didn't; the believers collectively heard the Spirit speak; and Paul *felt compelled* by the Holy Spirit. Even what they were doing when the Spirit communicated with them was different—Samuel was asleep! This isn't a formula, *it's a relationship.*

But it's easier to trust a formula than an unseen Spirit, isn't it? And so many believers will read these passages thinking, *If I just pray and fast enough . . . if I go to church and remain in worship . . . if I dedicate all my time to serving at the church. . . .* All of these pursuits are wonderful, but they are not the same thing as having a relationship with the Holy Spirit. A relationship strengthens and grows and changes over time. How and when the Spirit speaks to you will be different than your friends, because your relationship with him is unique. What you need to hear from him is an individual and special message for you.

There is a wonderful example of the Spirit speaking directly to an individual's need in the book of 1 Kings. The prophet Elijah had spent the past forty days running for his life when he found himself hiding in a cave at Mount Horeb—probably not where he thought or hoped the Lord was leading him. He'd been faithfully speaking out against the false prophets and idol worship in Israel, but when the evil queen Jezebel heard about it, she threatened him with death. He was tired, fearful, and despondent. But there in the cave, the Lord called him. "Come out to the mouth of the cave and experience my presence as I pass by."

Suddenly a powerful wind ripped through the mountains, shattering rocks and tearing the rocks apart, but the Scriptures tell us the Lord was not in the wind. After the wind came a mighty earthquake, but the Lord was not in the earthquake. Then ferocious fire roared through the mountain, but the Lord was not in the fire. "After the fire," the Bible says, "came a gentle whisper. When Elijah heard it, he pulled his cloak over his face and went out and stood at the mouth of the cave."[5]

God didn't show up or speak in all the ways we might have expected —a powerful wind, a mighty earthquake, a ferocious fire. He spoke in a gentle whisper, or as some translations say, a still small voice. Jesus said, "My sheep hear my voice."[6] But sometimes I wonder—*are we listening?* Are we listening for the gentle whisper of the Holy Spirit, or are we only looking for the powerful winds, mighty earthquakes, and ferocious fires?

Learning to recognize the Spirit's voice and trust the gentle whisper requires faith. It is letting go of the things we can see and control and stepping into the supernatural world. But the only way to walk with the Spirit is to trust him. To be vulnerable. To risk. "Today," the writer of Hebrews cautions us, "if you hear his voice, do not harden your hearts."[7]

GRACE, GRACE

After my experience at the Dennis Bennett event, my faith in Jesus began to grow. Guided by the Spirit, I read the Bible whenever I could. I read Christian books and listened to teachings on tape both at home and in the car. At the time, there was a radio station that played the sermons of J. Vernon McGee—he was so unlike anyone I had ever heard before! If there was a seminar or event at a local church, I was there. Whenever the church we were attending was open, I was there too. I was hungry for more of God, for the Word. I just couldn't get enough.

I developed a habit of praying each time I opened the Word. I would ask the Holy Spirit to bless me and reveal truth, and to help me understand what I was about to read. I asked him to open my mind to what the Scriptures were saying to me so that my thinking would be changed. Connie and I were still together and had joined a new ministry called Wind of the Spirit, led by pastors Larry and Audrey Eddings. Through their teaching, both Connie and I received so much healing. We spoke words of forgiveness to those who had failed us in the past, and also forgave ourselves. We sought out counseling. We were becoming closer and moving in the same direction spiritually, but after years of failed relationships and emotional trauma, we both had a lot of baggage.

Shortly after I first met Connie, we went away for a weekend together. We brought our two teenage sons and stayed in a lovely cabin near Crystal Mountain in Rainier National Park, Washington. The cabin backed right up to a wild and beautiful river full of white water and winter snowmelt. One afternoon, the boys and I stood at the river's edge, throwing rocks into the river.

"Let's build a raft!" I suggested.

The boys seemed excited and wanted to help, so we gathered up nearby driftwood and found some rope. We lashed some logs together, and after a while, we'd built a rather rough looking platform. The boys and I pushed it to the river's edge where it bobbed up and down on the water. It seemed like it might hold.

"Well, let's go!"

The two boys looked at me like I was crazy.

"I'm serious!" I said. "I'm going down the river on this."

The boys looked at the river, raging and churning up white water as it passed over the rocks. It was still winter, and rougher than usual.

"I'm not going," Danny said emphatically.

Not even my own son Steve was game. "No way."

"Well, I'm going to do it," I said emphatically.

At forty-three, and without an oar, I had no business being on this raft, but I was determined. I found a pole that I thought might work to steer. After a few quick tests, I realized it wouldn't work, but still, I wasn't deterred. *I need something to hang on to the raft in case I fall in*, I thought. The river was wild enough that I'd need the raft to keep myself afloat. Then the idea came to me. *I'll tie a rope around my ankle and attach it to the raft!* I didn't yet know the Lord, but God was with me in that moment. Even in my stupidity, he had a plan for me. He was waiting for me to come to him.

I hopped onto the raft, then tied the rope to my ankle as my safety connection in case I fell off. Then I shoved off from the shore. The current immediately pulled me out into the middle of the river. Try as I might, I could not steer the raft, which was quickly pulling me into a kind of log jam—piles of wood wedged up against a small island where white water pounded against it. I was entirely at the mercy of the river. In a matter of seconds, my raft collided with the logs and completely flipped over. The rear of raft went flying over me and I was suddenly trapped underneath.

The white water pummeled the raft without relief, pressing the raft into the island and keeping me pinned underwater together with logs and other stuck debris. *I can't get out!* Panic raced through me. Even if I could get a breath, the force of the current was actively pulling the raft into the island, and me along with it. *I'm still attached to the raft!* I gave a big push and somehow managed to get a quick a breath before being pulled under again. Now I had to untie the rope from my ankle. I fumbled around, and by some miracle, was able to break free and swim safely back to shore.

The Methodists call this *prevenient grace*. It's the unmerited favor of God on your life—his grace and mercy before you even knew him. But at the time, I didn't have a clue that God had preserved my life, I just knew I was lucky I hadn't died.

Shortly after I became a Christian, I remembered our weekend in the cabin by the river, and my ego that nearly killed me. And it hit me— God loved me so much that he preserved my life that weekend. He'd been right there with me, in my idiotic decision to tie myself to the raft, to get into the river . . . and he'd been there through my sin, my stupidity, and my rebellion. He kept me alive until the moment when I said yes to him. There's a comfort in knowing that God has always been with us. There's a comfort in grace—God's undeserved, unearned love for you and his favor on your life.

I think we sometimes struggle to hear the Spirit because we're so caught up in our past, weighed down by our sins and shame, still licking the wounds of our suffering, that we have a hard time opening ourselves up to the Spirit. We can't believe we are fully seen, loved, and totally forgiven. We need emotional and spiritual healing. God wants to lift our burdens and heal all of our wounds. It may not happen in a moment, but you will be changed. The Bible promises that. Where the Spirit of the Lord is, there is freedom.

REFLECTION & PRAYER

Sometimes when I'm praying with people who are stuck in past wounds, I will ask them to invite Jesus into the situation. With their eyes closed, I remind them that Jesus has always been with them, even before they knew him. If they can, I ask them to go back to that place, that room, that situation. *Can you see Jesus? Look around.* Quite often, there is something they want to keep covered or hidden, but to see Jesus in that place can be a comfort. He knows what you've been through.

I'll then ask them to look at Jesus. *What's he doing?* Sometimes he's crying and looking at them with love. Someone once told me he had his arms around them. He was going through it with them. I think about this a lot when I'm reminded of my own painful past, or when the enemy reminds me of things I'd rather forget. I try to let go of the shame and remember, Jesus was there, preserving me for the day I would become his child. And I let the grace of God comfort me in these wounds, and then turn that into comfort for others.

- If you need healing or if this has stirred something in you, I encourage you to talk to the Holy Spirit about it, and the elders of the church, if you're comfortable. Close your eyes and look for Jesus in those painful moments. Let the Spirit comfort and heal you.
- Are there areas in your past that you need to let go of? Moments of prevenient grace you need to accept? Spend time thanking the Spirit for his prevenient grace and mercy and give it back to him.
- There are many ways to listen to the Spirit. Sometimes he speaks to us through God's Word, and other times during prayer. From time to time, I'll hear a worship song and I can hear the Spirit using it to speak to me. Many times, another believer has shared something and is completely unaware that the Lord has used them to speak to me. God has even spoken to me through dreams. I encourage you to spend

time in worship, prayer, listening to good Bible teaching, reading the Word, speaking in tongues, and fellowshipping with other believers. You never know how the Spirit might speak to you!

- Take a moment to look back over the past few weeks. Has there been a moment when the Spirit was speaking, but you dismissed it? Is the Spirit speaking to you now? If so, I encourage you to respond. Take the next step.

- Build time into your life and schedule for the Spirit to move and work. Spend time with him!

CHAPTER 4

SPIRITUAL WARFARE

"Hey, good looking!"

Connie and I met while working together at Art Anderson Associates, a marine engineering company in Bremerton. Although I'd since left the company and we hadn't kept in touch, I recognized her voice immediately, even over the traffic and noise around the ferry terminal.

"When are you going to take me to dinner?" I teased, once I caught sight of her across the street. Just the sound of her voice lifted my spirits, and I suppose my vanity too. I'd just missed the ferry for a work trip to Seattle and had been feeling very much alone. My attempts at creating an "immediate family" in the States had ended badly. I had a few friends, but no family support, and no real community. To top it off, all the money I'd saved and brought with me from England was nearly gone. I jogged across the street to meet her.

"I don't know about dinner . . ." she said, a playful smile spreading across her face, "but how about a white-water rafting trip?" The Art Anderson Associates employees occasionally hosted group trips and there just happened to be one coming up. She filled me in on the rest of the details and a plan was made.

On our first date, we rafted down white-water rapids on the Methow River in eastern Washington. It was the perfect day, and we had a great time. On the way back to Bremerton, we stopped by the roadside and strolled along a beautiful, sparkling creek. Connie knew all the names of the flowers and told me about them as we walked. We both enjoyed being in nature and talked easily. I was hooked. Looking back, I was probably hoping this new relationship would heal me of all that had gone wrong in the previous ones. But that's never how it works, is it?

Connie and I were married about a year later. By that time, I had accepted Christ and we were both walking with the Lord. We were growing together spiritually, but still carrying around all the trauma from our previous broken relationships. Connie, for her part, heard some teachings on codependency and began going to a counselor, which in my view, only led to more problems in our relationship. Her pendulum had swung from an unhealthy codependency to being so totally independent that she was almost impossible to live with.

I, on the other hand, tended to run roughshod over my partners. When I made up my mind about something, I went for it. There was no discussion or consideration for my partner. I was often angry and could be a bully when I wanted to get my own way. In hindsight, I see that the Holy Spirit was teaching each of us to come to him first, but it wasn't an easy lesson. The Holy Spirit was teaching Connie to be led by him in important decisions rather than be manipulated by me. Meanwhile, he was teaching me to run to him when I felt rejected and abandoned by Connie as she learned to trust the Lord herself.

On one particularly frustrating evening, I opened up to our small group. "She won't even listen to me. We can't even have a conversation about things," I complained. "Every time I try to talk to her, she tells me she doesn't care to hear what I have to say!"

I was frustrated and didn't know what to do. I hoped that because we were both Christians, this relationship would be different than the previous ones. Connie and I had both attended Gary Smalley's Love Is a Decision Conference, so divorce wasn't an option. But our marriage was far from easy. I loved Connie, and I was desperate to make the relationship work, but the situation had become insurmountable.

Connie's counselor worked with another church, but she attended our small group. "This is part of the process that Connie must go through to become healthy," she gently explained. "You need to patiently experience what she's going through and work with her. And you're going to need to do your own work with a counselor to learn how to manage your anger."

Then she gave me the best relationship advice I've ever received. "You can't love Connie as she is now in your own love. It's got to be the love of Jesus. Your love just won't be able to do it." She finished by praying for an outpouring of the Holy Spirit on my life, so that I would be able to love Connie as she needed to be loved at that time.

LED BY THE HOLY SPIRIT

When Jesus was baptized by John, Luke tells us that "the Holy Spirit descended on him in bodily form, like a dove; and a voice came from heaven, 'You are my beloved Son; with you I am well pleased.'"[1] This was the beginning of Jesus' public ministry. But what happens next seems strange. Jesus—full of the Holy Spirit—was "led by the Spirit in the wilderness for forty days" where he was tempted by the devil.[2]

I don't like to talk about spiritual warfare very much. I think some people give the devil too much credit, and others forget we've been given power over the spiritual authorities. Still, spiritual warfare is scriptural and throughout the New Testament, we are warned to stay on guard and be alert. The devil does not want you and me walking in the power of the Holy Spirit and will do whatever he can to block, discourage, and confuse you. But don't worry. Jesus has already defeated him.

Let's read through Luke's account of how the devil tried to tempt Jesus:

And Jesus, full of the Holy Spirit, returned from the Jordan and was led by the Spirit in the wilderness for forty days, being tempted by the devil. And he ate nothing during those days. And when they were ended, he was hungry. The devil said to him, "If you are the Son of God, command this stone to become bread." And Jesus answered him, "It is written, 'Man shall not live by bread alone.'"[3]

When the devil came to tempt Jesus, Jesus was alone in the wilderness, and had been fasting for forty days. He was hungry and no doubt lonely. *Take care of yourself*, Satan says. *If you're really God, you can turn these stones into bread. You don't have to wait for God or trust God to do it for you.* But Jesus doesn't take the bait—he doesn't need to prove himself to Satan. Jesus knows who he is.

And the devil took him up and showed him all the kingdoms of the world in a moment of time, and said to him, "To you I will give all this authority and their glory, for it has been delivered to me, and I give it to whom I will. If you, then, will worship me, it will all be yours." And Jesus answered him, "It is written, "'You shall worship the Lord your God, and him only shall you serve.'"[4]

In his second attempt, Satan shows Jesus all the kingdoms of the world, *This could be yours*, he says. *You don't need God. I can give you everything—all the kingdoms of the world.* But again, Jesus doesn't fall for Satan's tricks. He doesn't argue with him. He simply responds with God's Word. One day, every knee and every kingdom will bow before Jesus, but he's going to do it God's way—through the cross—not the cheap trick Satan is promising.

And he took him to Jerusalem and set him on the pinnacle of the temple and said to him, "If you are the Son of God, throw yourself down from here, for it is written, "'He will command his angels concerning you, to guard you,' and "'On their hands they will bear you up, lest you strike your foot against a stone.'"

And Jesus answered him, "It is said, 'You shall not put the Lord your God to the test.'"[5]

Now Satan's going for the final test. *If God loves you that much, prove it. Throw yourself down and let's see what happens.* But Jesus doesn't have to prove it. He already knows the love of the Father.

It's interesting that these are many of the same lies Satan throws at believers today. They are subtle deceptions designed to cause you to doubt. Not much has changed from the Garden of Eden when Satan asked Eve, *Did God really say . . . ?* Perhaps you've heard some version of this yourself.

Why wait for God when you can take care of things yourself?
Maybe God doesn't love you as much as you think he does.
Why would God lead me out here to the wilderness?

PRAYERS OF DELIVERANCE

As Connie worked through her codependency, and I struggled to love her with the love of Jesus, I knew I had to deal with some of my own issues. I was in counseling, but it felt as though something was holding back my spiritual growth and blocking the work of the Spirit flowing out of me. I wanted to be free. After talking with some of the lay ministers with Wind of the Spirit Ministries, they agreed to pray with me; they felt my spiritual block may be due to experiences I had before I was saved. Although I was no longer engaged in those activities, it seemed as though Satan had obtained a foothold.

A few nights later, we met to pray. The men explained that I needed *deliverance prayer*—prayer that would enable Jesus to reveal the truth of my spiritual condition and cleanse me from any evil influence. I was nervous. I'd never heard of deliverance prayer, but I trusted them, and more importantly, I trusted Jesus. I knew that they would talk with him before they prayed for me.

The men began to pray, and as they did, Jesus began revealing things to me that were holding me back in my walk with him. I saw images, or maybe visions. At first, I saw all sorts of horrible things—things I'd done and seen—and I began pressing them down into a garbage can filled with flames. As the flames grew higher and hotter, I grabbed the lid and slammed it onto the can, successfully putting out the fire. A little smoke seeped out, but nothing more escaped.

At this point, the men praying for me paused, and began talking with one another about what to do next. It sounded as though they weren't very experienced with deliverance prayer and weren't sure how to proceed. Nevertheless, they decided to continue in prayer, asking the Holy Spirit for guidance, and as they did, I had another vision.

This time, I saw the tomb where Jesus was buried. I walked in and saw white robes on the floor; a black sheet hung on the wall. I could tell the black sheet was covering something, so I pulled it off, revealing a skeleton with an evil face. It was terrifying! One of the men told me to knock it off the wall and smash it completely, and so I did; trampling it under my feet until the skeleton was ground to dust. I was wiping my foot over the dust when I saw the same evil face smiling at me with its hideous grin. I erased the image with my foot and it was gone. With that, the prayer came to a close.

I was tired but felt a sense of relief. It was as if a huge load had been lifted off of my back. Afterwards, the men and I talked about the images I'd seen while they prayed. I concluded that the hideous grin—Satan's face—was a reminder that he is defeated, but still roaming about looking to deceive, kill, and destroy. I went home that evening knowing that I'd been set free, and that by the blood of Jesus I'd overcome, but also determined to stay alert, be on guard, and keep praying in the Spirit.

GREATER IS HE WHO IS IN US

You will encounter spiritual warfare when you walk with Jesus and as you lean into a life filled with the Holy Spirit. This was true for the early church and it's still true for us today. Even Peter—who walked on water with Jesus and preached a message where three-thousand people got saved—was tempted and tried by Satan. He denied Jesus three times. In his letter to the church, Peter reminds us:

> Humble yourselves, therefore, under the mighty hand of God so that at the proper time he may exalt you, casting all your anxieties on him, because he cares for you. Be sober-minded; be watchful. Your adversary the devil prowls around like a roaring lion, seeking someone to devour. Resist him, firm in your faith, knowing that the same kinds of suffering are being experienced by your brotherhood throughout the world.[6]

Peter knew what it was to be tempted. We like to think we're above it, but we aren't. *Humble yourselves,* Peter said. *Be sober-minded; be watchful. The enemy is real!* But Peter also knew what it was to be restored. *Cast your cares on God,* he encourages us, *because he cares for you.* James put it a little more bluntly: "Submit yourselves therefore to God. Resist the devil, and he will flee from you."[7]

Over the years, I've prayed a simple prayer whenever I'm feeling frustrated by situations or experiences. "I resist you Satan. You have no authority here. You must flee." Is it spiritual warfare? I don't always know. Rather than focus on evil, I lift my prayers and requests with thanksgiving to God.

Paul tells us in the book of Ephesians that our real battle isn't with other people, but "against the spiritual forces of evil in the heavenly places."[8] Therefore, we must put on the whole armor of God, and take up the shield of faith, with which we can extinguish the fiery darts of the enemy, the sword of the Spirit which is the Word of God, and the helmet of salvation, praying at all times in the Spirit.[9] He exhorts us not to be anxious about this, "but in everything by prayer and supplication with thanksgiving let [our] requests be made known to God. And the peace of God, which surpasses all understanding, will guard [our] hearts and [our] minds in Christ Jesus."[10]

When the world seems to be falling apart, when your problems are bigger than your faith, when your past threatens to destroy your future, and when difficult relationships challenge you—submit yourself to God. Jesus has defeated our enemy and he's given us authority over our enemy. Jesus said, "do not rejoice in this, that the spirits are subject to you, but rejoice that your names are written in heaven."[11] We have a real enemy, but more importantly, we have a mighty Savior who loves us, cares about us, and has already overcome. And best of all—his Spirit lives within us.

"Little children, you are from God and have overcome them, for he who is in you is greater than he who is in the world."[12]

Reflection & Prayer

I've thought a lot about the advice to love Connie where she was and as she was, not with my love, but with the love of Jesus. It wasn't easy, and we did struggle. The Holy Spirit was working on me too! After some time, Connie's pendulum of absolute independence came back down to a balanced middle ground, and with God's help my anger receded, and we've enjoyed a good relationship ever since. But it reminds me that we each have stories of emotional healing and freedom that often involve transitional periods, which can be difficult to manage.

We don't always know if it's spiritual warfare or the old nature trying to resurrect itself. It can be difficult to discern what's happening in the spiritual realm. That's why it's so important that we continue to pray in the Spirit.

> For we do not know what to pray for as we ought, but the Spirit himself intercedes for us with groanings too deep for words. And he who searches hearts knows what is the mind of the Spirit, because the Spirit intercedes for the saints according to the will of God.[13]

- If you feel you are still stuck in old habits or are being held back by some of the trauma and baggage from your past, talk to the Holy Spirit. Ask him to reveal to you what is holding you back. Ask him if there is anything in you that he wants to heal.

- When the Holy Spirit reveals areas where you are struggling or need healing, start talking with Jesus about those things. Make it a priority. Is there any unforgiveness in your life? Ask others to pray for you and with you. Go to elders at your church and ask them to lay hands on you and anoint you with oil.

- We'll talk more about healing and restoration in relationships in the next chapter, but for now, who do you need to be patient with? What relationships can you entrust to the Holy Spirit and walk patiently alongside as he does the work that only he can do? Who do you need the Spirit's help to love? Ask the Holy Spirit to fill you to overflowing now.

CHAPTER 5

FOLLOWING THE SPIRIT'S LEAD

Within a year of being married, Connie and I were blessed with a daughter—Brittany. Though she was a surprise to us both, we soon began to see her arrival as a blessing. Brittany made us into a family, blending together our lives and children. Her presence solidified our commitment to make our marriage work.

That's not to say it was easy. Connie and I were in our forties!* Plus, Brittany refused to sleep for the first year of her life, adding considerable stress to an already difficult situation. It was an adjustment for everyone, especially our two boys. We were newly married, new believers, new parents and new stepparents, and we were learning how to trust God together.

On top of all that, I was unemployed.

Before I moved to the States, I worked in England as a technical illustrator, a graphic designer, and a three-dimensional designer (the closest I ever came to my mother's dream of me being an architect). I

---

* When Connie was pregnant with Brittany, we suddenly found ourselves surrounded by ten other couples over forty, who were also pregnant. What a joy it was! We called ourselves the OPEC fellowship group—Older People Expecting Children. After Brittany arrived, we called it Older People Enjoying Children.

designed trade show exhibits, interpretive centers, museums, permanent displays, and touring exhibits for the British government. Eventually I changed direction and became a project manager for the Central Office of Information, working on exhibits in the UK, Europe, and Southeast Asia. When my boss asked if I'd like to manage a project in the US, I jumped at the chance. I'd never even heard of Seattle, Washington!

In Seattle, I managed an exhibit by the London-based Design Center, featuring British products and creative services as part of a government effort to increase global awareness around Britain as a creative force in the world.* I'd enjoyed my previous jobs in other countries, but not having to deal with a language barrier was wonderful. One day while setting up the exhibit, I noticed a familiar face among the new installation team from Texas. He recognized me too. Turns out we'd gone to Kingston Tech together over twenty-five years earlier! Like all good Englishmen, Roger and I met over a glass of beer, laughing and sharing how we'd each come to be in Seattle.

When the exhibit closed a few months later, I wasn't ready to leave. I'd fallen in love with the Pacific Northwest—the water, the majestic Olympic and Cascade Mountains, the noisy, outspoken, and transparent Americans, and the way Washingtonians maintain lane discipline on the freeway. And now, there was a new woman in my life. We'd met at a party Roger had invited me to and spent the night together. The next morning, she asked if I'd like to go to church. Shocked as I was (what an odd thing to ask a man you just met!), I said yes. I had nothing to lose.

My first experience at Silverdale United Methodist Church was like nothing I'd ever experienced before. I knew very little about Christianity or a charismatic worship gathering, but I knew what I felt—I sensed the very presence of God. It was like a spiritual awakening, although I must admit, all the hugs and welcomes made me a bit uncomfortable. Still, I

---

* The exhibit I was managing was part of a store promotion of British products at the Frederick and Nelson store in downtown Seattle. I was helping with advertising and press coverage.

enjoyed the service and went back a few more times. I was drawn to the place, and hoped I might see Donna again.

But after those few short months in Seattle, my work project ended, and my work-visa expired. I returned to London and settled back into my lifeless suburban flat—a far cry from the hotel and expense account I had in Seattle—and missed the life I'd come to love in Seattle. With no accountability and very little responsibility, it wasn't a reality, but I bought into it anyway. I told my boss I was resigning, and sold or gave away my things. With only a suitcase and two boxes, I moved back to Seattle.

As it turns out, a new life, a new family, and a second marriage in Seattle had not been the answer to my problems. By the time Connie and I met, I was divorced a second time and unemployed. But Connie and I were different. We wanted to walk by faith and trust God, and so —though it didn't make sense with teenagers and a newborn living in our small, rented home—when the next unemployment check came, we gave ten percent of our income to the church as a tithe.

WALKING BY FAITH

Even the disciples, who daily spent time with Jesus in the flesh, had to learn to walk by faith. They had to put their trust in him, though it didn't make sense to their natural minds. Trust is the basis of any healthy relationship. But it's one thing to say, "I believe the Holy Spirit speaks," and quite another to act upon an instinct or a thought that just might be Holy Spirit speaking to you. And still quite another to tithe on an unemployment check! The disciples experienced these same growing pains, and they were with Jesus every day.

"Where shall we buy bread for these people to eat?" Jesus asked Philip. A large crowd of some five thousand people (probably more with the women and children) was approaching, eager to hear Jesus speak. It was late in the afternoon, and they were in a remote place. The other disciples had already suggested Jesus send them away to get food before it got too late.

Philip ran some quick numbers in his head, "It would take more than half a year's wages to buy enough bread for each one to have a bite!"

The miracle of Jesus feeding the five thousand is found in all four Gospels, but only John lets us in on a secret: Jesus already knew what he was going to do. This wasn't a math quiz for Philip, but a test of faith.[1] Philip is the practical, think-it-through version of us. *How are we going to do this? Well, let me run some numbers and I'll let you know.* That's how most of us respond when we first hear the Spirit's voice.

That's not possible. The math doesn't add up.

That can't be God, right?

God, I can't do that!!

That churning in my gut must just be what I had for lunch.

Walking with the Lord requires faith. Not only will you doubt if the Spirit is speaking to you, but you'll need faith to act on what he's saying.

After the death and resurrection of Jesus, the Spirit spoke to Philip again saying, "Go south to the road—the desert road—that goes down from Jerusalem to Gaza."

The Holy Spirit spoke to Philip, but let's not skim over his specific instructions.

"Go." That's it.

Go to the road that leads to Gaza.

Go to the store down the street from your house.

Go to the boardwalk where it intersects with the main road.

This time Philip didn't ask questions or provide feedback—he acted on what he heard. His faith had grown since he saw Jesus feed the crowd of five thousand people with nothing more than five barley loaves and two small fish. Philip went, and the Scriptures tell us that *on his way* he met an Ethiopian eunuch who was traveling home from Jerusalem where he'd been worshipping. When Philip came across him, the eunuch was "sitting in his chariot reading the Book of Isaiah the prophet."[2]

So far, nothing unusual has happened. Philip was *on the way* to where the Spirit directed him when he noticed a chariot.

"The Spirit told Philip, 'Go to that chariot and stay near it.'"[3]

Now that Philip's on the way, now that he's moving, the Spirit gives him more instruction. But he didn't tell Philip what to say, or what would happen next. The next instruction was as simple as the first. *Stand near that chariot.* Following the Spirit's instructions, Philip overheard the man reading aloud from the prophet Isaiah. So, he engaged the man with a logical question, "Do you understand what you're reading?"

This single encounter opened the door for Philip to share the good news of Jesus' death and resurrection with this man, who—it is believed—took the gospel back to his homeland of Ethiopia.

TRUST IS AN ACT OF FAITH

Connie and I hadn't been married long when someone in our small group told us about tithing. They directed us to the following Scripture in Malachi 3:

> Return to me, and I will return to you, says the LORD of hosts. But you say, "How shall we return?" Will man rob God? Yet you are robbing me. But you say, "How have we robbed you?" In your tithes and contributions. You are cursed with a curse, for you are robbing me, the whole nation of you. Bring the full tithe into the storehouse, that there may be food in my house.[4]

I was stunned when I read those words. We're robbing God when we don't tithe on what he's provided? Wow. I did not want to rob God. In the next verse, God tells us that we can put him to the test on this. I believe this is the only place in Scripture where it is suggested that we can test God. "And thereby put me to the test, says the LORD of hosts, if I will not open the windows of heaven for you and pour down for you a blessing until there is no more need."[5] It's almost hard to believe. *I dare you to try it!* God says. *I dare you to tithe and see if I won't bless you!*

Tithing may not seem like part of experiencing the Holy Spirit in your life, but I think it is paramount. When we tithe, we are actively putting our trust in God and looking to him to provide for our needs. It's not about the money, it's about changing the attitude of our heart. If everything we have is from God, then even our income, our savings, and our finances are his. We are the managers, the stewards—not the owners. Just like we are stewards of the spiritual gifts he's given us.

Luke tells us that one day while Jesus was standing in the Temple with his disciples, he watched as the wealthy people dropped their offering or their tithes into the collection box. Then a poor widow walked up and dropped in her two small coins. "I tell you the truth," Jesus said as the woman walked away, "this poor widow has given more than all the rest of them. For they have given a tiny part of their surplus, but she, poor as she is, has given everything she has."[6]

Connie and I were in a transitional stage of our Christian lives, learning to trust God in all things. Through reading our Bibles, attending church, and in our small groups, we were beginning to understand the very nature of God as our loving heavenly Father. He loves us, he cares for us, and he's adopted us as his children—of course he will provide for us! As Paul writes in the book of Romans, "For all who are led by the Spirit of God are sons of God. For you did not receive the spirit of slavery to fall back into fear, but you have received the Spirit of adoption as sons, by whom we cry, 'Abba! Father!'"[7]

"Should we tithe on our gross or net income?" I asked Pastor Larry one day.

"Well," he said, thinking for a moment. "What do you want to be blessed on?"

Our first tithe was on my unemployment check, which wasn't much. Still, giving ten percent of our gross earnings took faith. But the thing is, you can't out-give God. And when you start to give, you open yourself up to receiving more. It's not a transactional giving and receiving, but an overflow of gratitude. When you get blessed by God, you give back out of thankfulness. You want to be a blessing to others.

"Give, and it will be given to you." Jesus said. "Good measure, pressed down, shaken together, running over, will be put into your lap. For with the measure you use it will be measured back to you."[8]

WE CAN TRUST THE HOLY SPIRIT

Not long after we began tithing, the Lord blessed me with a design job in Seattle. The work was challenging and the commute was long, but we were grateful. Connie and I continued faithfully tithing on whatever the Lord gave us, and God continued to renew our minds as we gave, blessing us both spiritually and financially.

We were living in a small beach cabin on Dyes Inlet that Connie had been renting since before we were married. It was old, drafty, and small, but the location was wonderful. We loved it. Connie and I dreamt of buying the cabin and remodeling it to fit our growing family. With the help of church friends and Connie's stepdad, we'd already modified the basement for our two boys. I was making a decent income, but we really couldn't afford to buy it. My income was just enough for us to live on, and we didn't have any money to save.

Still, we prayed. And one day (in faith or just for fun, I don't know which) we asked Bill, the owner, if he'd consider selling.

"No," he said without any hesitation. "It's not for sale. You can't afford to buy it anyway."

A few days later, Bill's wife Rosy surprised us with a phone call. She wanted to know if we were still interested in buying the cabin. We could hardly believe it, but Bill was right—we couldn't afford it even if they were willing to sell.

"Lord," we prayed. "If it's your will for us to buy this place, then you need to make a way."

Rosy and Bill offered to sell the cabin for $135,000, which was below the market value. I have no idea why he changed his mind. It was a great price, but it was still over our budget, not to mention the money needed for a deposit and closing costs. We continued to pray. Strangely, we felt sure the Lord wanted us to buy it; we just didn't know how he would pull it off.

A few days later, Rosy called again.

Once again, Connie, Brittany, and I went to meet with Bill and Rosy. Bill was a gruff old Scandinavian guy who wasn't much for conversation. He would listen, tell you what he thought, and then the discussion would come to an abrupt end. But he always warmed up when our daughter Brittany was around. She toddled her way over to him and his hard exterior melted as he picked her up and gently sat her on his knee.

"Bill and I talked," Rosy said, "And we can drop the price to $100,000 . . . we're also willing to carry the contract, so you won't have to go to the bank for a loan."

Connie and I looked at each other, completely stunned. Then we directed our attention back to Rosy and Bill, who was completely distracted by Brittany. I started to interject, but Rosy wouldn't let me.

"We'll set the interest a full point below the current rate . . ." she continued, "and we'll give you a rebate for last year's rent so you have money for the down payment and to cover the closing costs."

We hadn't even had a moment to compose ourselves or respond, when Bill set Brittany down and turned toward us.

"This is ridiculous," he said, suddenly agitated. He stood up from the table where we were sitting. "This makes absolutely no sense. I can't do this!"

"Bill . . . ?" Rosy sputtered, her face reddening. She tried to reason with him, but he was adamant.

"No," he said, walking away. "No deal."

We left in tears. Our hopes dashed.

"Lord, if this is your will. Please make a way."

Rosy called again the next day. "I'm so sorry about Bill's outburst yesterday," she began, "but we really do want you to have the house. We're going to sell it to you for $98,000."

God had done the impossible. Not long after, the papers were drawn up and signed, and we became the happy homeowners of a small beach cabin on Dyes Inlet. Connie and I have continued to tithe faithfully, but after our early experiences, it has become less of an obligation, and more an outpouring of gratitude to God and an appreciation of his presence in our lives. He's been so good to us.

REFLECTION & PRAYER

In one of the Pharisee's attempts to condemn Jesus, they asked him whether or not they—Jewish citizens under Roman rule—should pay taxes to Caesar. It was a trick. They knew if he answered to pay taxes to Caesar, the people would revolt; and if he told them they didn't need to pay taxes to Caesar, Rome would lock him up. Instead, Jesus asked them to bring him a coin.

"Whose picture and inscription are on the coin?" Jesus asked.

"Caesar's," they all replied.

"Well, then," Jesus said, "give to Caesar what belongs to Caesar, and give to God what belongs to God."[9]

Our very lives belong to God. We owe him everything we have.

- In what ways has God blessed you? Lift up your voice and pray, sing, and praise in the Spirit. Thank him for what he has done.
- Are there any areas in your life where you have been holding back from God? Perhaps out of a lack of trust, or fear? If the Spirit has brought something to mind, confess that to him now. Ask him to help you trust him and walk in faith.
- Do you want to grow deeper in your relationship with the Holy Spirit? Test God in your tithing. I dare you to try!
- Has the Spirit put something on your heart—a dream or the hope of something else that seems impossible and out of reach? Trust him! Ask and act according to the Spirit's response.

CHAPTER 6

FORGIVENESS

S hortly after I was born—in keeping with English tradition—I was christened at our local parish church in Sandhurst, England. It was 1941 and our world was full of air raids, bombs, and rations. My mother would later tell me that only after the young vicar began the service, did he realize there was no water in the font to christen me with. The war had affected everything, even the church.

"Where is the holy water?" the vicar asked, nervously scanning the room.

Not one for religious ceremony, my grandfather yelled, "It's in the river Jordan, boy!"

My father had died in the war, leaving my mother with a two-year-old son, and me—still in her womb. She moved into the Cashmore family home shortly after my father's death, but fled when my grandfather made sexual advances toward her. Sometime after I was born, she married my dad's brother Ron, and they moved to Southwest London. Ron served in the Royal Navy and was gone most of the time until the war ended when I was about four years old.

During that time, our home was not far from the West Surrey Regiment's headquarters in Kingston and the military barracks in Richmond Park. Consequently, we were frequent targets for German bombing raids, and later, the Doodlebugs fired from Northern France about one hundred miles away. The Doodlebugs were essentially an unmanned flying bomb—when the front propeller reached a certain number of pre-timed revolutions, it would cut the engine and begin free-falling from the sky. If you could hear the bomb's motor, you were safe. Only when things went quiet did we have to run for cover. We lived in a constant state of fear and panic, and spent many nights in an air-raid shelter.

Due to bomb damage, we were forced to move at least three times during the war. For a while, we lived in the countryside with my mother's sister, Chris, and her family of four boys. Her willingness to invite us into her very small house was really quite significant. After the bombings ended, we moved back to Kingston, staying with Aunt Sybil at first, and later with Aunt May. Somehow, in the midst of all this, my mother gave birth to my younger brother, Michael.

After the war, Ron did menial work, at times working two or three jobs. Still, he struggled to provide the kind of lifestyle my mother demanded. They were not well-suited. If she wanted something, she got it.* I've often wondered whether my mother really loved Ron or if she simply married him out of necessity. They were always fighting or arguing about something, leaving Ron resentful and even hostile toward us kids.

My mother cooked us breakfast to order every day—poached, fried, or boiled eggs, depending on our mood. "Just give 'em all the same!" Ron would grumble, but she wouldn't budge. She gave us all of her time, energy, and attention, much to Ron's annoyance, and I think, neglect. He would regularly complain about this and told us many times, "I work so hard for you and you're not even my kids!"

---

* My mother loved to buy us Harris Tweed overcoats for winter; I'm sure Ron thought there was a much less expensive product we could be wearing.

As the years went by, Ron's resentment and anger grew. His jealousy and suspicion of any man my mother was friendly with—the insurance agent who came once a month to collect a premium, the shopkeeper who sold her groceries—often turned violent. Over time, their arguments grew more heated, and he became aggressive. You could feel the tension building. We walked around on tiptoe, trying to avoid setting off the landmines, but we had no idea where they were. Anything could set him off.

On one particularly tense evening, we all sat at the table as mom laid out the evening meal. Without thinking, I began humming quietly under my breath.

"Cut it out!" Ron yelled, shooting an annoyed look my way. He was ready to explode.

We all jumped when he yelled and then tried to sit very still, our eyes fixed on our plates in front of us. But the humming continued. I didn't even realize I was doing it. Looking back, I'm sure it was my body's way of coping; trying to self soothe in the midst of a very tense situation.

Ron flew into a rage. "I said, cut it out!" he barked.

"Oh, leave him alone . . ." my mother started to interject. But it was too late. The table was already flying across the room. Dishes and plates crashed to the floor. I can still see the gravy sliding down the wall and the remains of our dinner scattered across the room. And then we all disappeared. That's just how it was.

When I was a teenager, Ron charged at me after I'd done something to upset him. I don't remember what. I flew up the stairs as quickly as I could with Ron right on my heels. I ran into my room and locked the door behind me. Although he'd broken doors off hinges before, this particular door was quite heavy, so I felt secure with it locked. Ron banged on the door.

"Open up!" he growled. "I want to talk to you."

My mother ran up the stairs and was now on the landing with Ron. I could hear their emotional exchange, her speaking softly to him, and for once, not provoking an already explosive situation. Neighbors had called the police on previous occasions, so perhaps she was trying to avoid another house call.

"I just want to talk to you." Ron repeated, in a carefully measured tone. "Open the door."

"Yes, Bobby," my mother pleaded. "Let us in."

I waited a while and—against my better judgment—slowly opened the door. Crack! Ron's fist flew through the opening and hit me full in the face, knocking me clear across the room. I was stunned. He'd said he just wanted to talk. That was the last time I trusted Ron and really, anyone else in my family.

If ever I become a father, I vowed to myself, *I will never do what he did to me.*

WHAT WE HOLD ON TO

When Peter asked Jesus about forgiveness, Jesus responded with a story about a king reconciling his accounts. The king called in all the servants who owed him money and found one who owed millions of dollars. When the servant couldn't pay his debt, the king ordered he be sold— along with his wife, children, and everything he owned. "Please," the servant begged, falling to his knees before the king, "please, be patient with me, and I will pay it all." Moved with pity, the king released the man and forgave his debt.

But this same man went to a fellow servant who owed him a few thousand dollars—a small fraction of what the man had owed the king —and demanded his fellow servant pay the debt in full. "Please be patient with me," the servant pleaded, "and I will pay it all." But the man would hear nothing more. He had his fellow servant arrested and placed in prison until he could pay in full.

When the king heard what the man had done, he called him back in. "You evil servant!" the king said. "I forgave you that tremendous debt because you pleaded with me. Shouldn't you have mercy on your fellow servant, just as I had mercy on you?"[1] Then the king sent the man to prison to be tortured until he had paid his debt in full.

When Jesus was finished telling the story, he turned to his disciples and said, "That's what my heavenly Father will do to you if you refuse to forgive your brothers and sisters from your heart."[2]

We tend to hang onto stuff—past wounds, unforgiveness, shame, resentment, anger—because we think it's not that significant. Perhaps we don't want to own the hurt because that would make us responsible for working through it and seeking healing or reconciliation. You may feel you have a right to hold onto it, but Jesus takes unforgiveness very seriously. When Jesus taught the disciples how to pray, he said, "if you forgive others their trespasses, your heavenly Father will also forgive you, but if you do not forgive others their trespasses, neither will your Father forgive your trespasses."[3]

But sometimes, the issue isn't about forgiving other people—it's about forgiving ourselves. "If we confess our sins," John the Beloved wrote, "he is faithful and just to forgive us our sins and to cleanse us from all unrighteousness."[4] When we hold onto our past—sins that God has already forgiven us for—we limit our ability to receive God's unconditional love and grace for ourselves. He hasn't just forgiven our sins, Psalm 103 tells us, he has completely removed them, as far as the east is from the west.[5]

MORE RIGHTEOUS THAN THE PHARISEES

Since the fall of man, God has been in the business of pursuing and restoring us into a right relationship with him. First, he gave us the law, the Ten Commandments through Moses. We can't live up to the law, and the law can't save us. It was never intended to. The law only shows us how desperately we need a Savior. Thank God we have been saved by grace through the death and resurrection of Jesus Christ! Still, there are consequences of actions—sin leaves a mark. We live in a fallen world.

During the Sermon on the Mount, Jesus told those gathered around that he hadn't come to abolish God's law, but to fulfill it. "For I tell you, unless your righteousness exceeds that of the scribes and Pharisees, you will never enter the kingdom of heaven."[6] The Pharisees were the Jewish keepers of the religious law. They saw to it that the people abided by God's commandments. But who could be *more righteous* than the Pharisees? They had added hundreds of additional laws to the original ten God had given Moses.

To emphasize the point, Jesus continued, "You have heard that it was said to those of old, 'You shall not murder; and whoever murders will be liable to judgment.'" Of course, they'd all heard about the sixth commandment—you shall not murder. Jesus continued, "But I say to you that everyone who is angry with his brother will be liable to judgment; whoever insults his brother will be liable to the council; and whoever says, 'You fool!' will be liable to the hell of fire."[7]

This is the standard that exceeds the righteousness of the Pharisees —it's not only our behavior that matters, but *the attitude of our hearts.* You may not have had an affair, but if you've lusted after someone, then you've broken the commandment. You may not have stolen, but if you coveted in your heart, you've already broken the law. This is the standard that exceeds the Pharisee's righteousness—the standard needed to enter the kingdom of heaven. But who can keep that law? No one.

In the book of Galatians, Paul asks, "Why, then, was the law given? It was given alongside the promise to show people their sins."[8] Jesus didn't come to abolish the law, but to fulfill it. In his life, he followed the law perfectly, outwardly and inwardly, and in his death, his paid the price for our sins completely. And the same is true for those who have sinned against us. We are the ones who have been forgiven millions by the king, and yet still demand that others pay the thousands they owe to us.

The Jewish Christians in the church of Galatia had a similar problem. They wanted all the new male believers to be circumcised; a requirement of the law they were born into. They wanted to hold others to a standard they'd not been able to keep. But Paul challenged them, saying, "Did you receive the Spirit by works of the law or by hearing with faith? Are you so foolish? Having begun by the Spirit, are you now being perfected by the flesh?"[9] After being saved by grace, not their own works, they were looking to their good works to keep them in a right relationship with the Father.

Unforgiveness—holding others to account, while wanting grace for ourselves—is holding us back from truly experiencing the unfathomable mercy and grace of God. "See to it," the book of Hebrews says, "that no one fails to obtain the grace of God; that no 'root of bitterness' springs up and causes trouble, and by it many become defiled."[10] Our old coping mechanisms and mindsets aren't helping us in this new life— they're hurting us. Unforgiveness has poisoned our hearts and dried up the holy font leaving us to wonder like the young vicar, "Where is the holy water? Where is the grace of God?"

We are forgiven! We are loved! But we need the Comforter to heal to our wounds. We need to forgive.

THE NEED FOR FORGIVENESS

By now, Connie and I were a few years into marriage and doing well. We each put a lot of prayer, therapy, and effort into our relationship and were both growing spiritually. We'd also joined a new small group, led by Jack and Ruby Langel. Our Monday night group was a special place for me. There were believers from Silverdale United Methodist Church, Wind of the Spirit, and a whole cross-section of other churches, which gave us a wonderful variety of viewpoints and added depth to our discussions. I found a lot of healing there. Jack and Ruby became my spiritual parents and discipled me for many years.

One evening, after a teaching on forgiveness, I opened up to the group about my stepfather Ron. More than twenty years had passed, and yet, the pain and hurt he caused were still fresh in my mind.

"Is he still alive?" Ruby asked.

I knew he was still alive and told her so, but I didn't know how to contact him or where he was. I didn't want to know. Not long after he punched me in the face, I moved out. I hadn't seen him since. A friend's family took me in for a while until I finished school, but I'd felt like a burden. I was only sixteen years old.

"I think you need to find out where he's living and go forgive him," Ruby said softly.

Ron was aggressive, temperamental, and scary. I spent my childhood terrified of him. He caused so much pain and brokenness, and now . . . I was being asked to forgive him? It was unthinkable. I did not want to do it.

"I'm sorry for what you've been through, Bob. I really am. But the Holy Spirit has put this strongly on my heart," Ruby said, her words full of love. "You need to forgive him."

When I first got saved, it was deeply evident to me that I was a sinner. I needed Jesus to forgive me and set me free. I received his sacrifice on the cross as the payment for my sin. I believed that my sin was forgiven and forgotten. But that night, the Holy Spirit revealed, through another believer who cared deeply for me, that it wasn't really forgotten. Not for me anyway. God had forgiven and forgotten my sin, yes, but I hadn't forgotten nor forgiven Ron's. I did not want to forgive him, but I needed to.

REFLECTION & PRAYER

Over the years, I've prayed with many individuals—many of them long-time Christians—who were shocked to discover they were holding on to unforgiveness. It was buried so deep in their hearts; they weren't even aware of its presence. The prophet Jeremiah wrote, "The heart is deceitful above all things, and desperately sick; who can understand it?"[11]

Sometimes a loved one has pointed out that their emotional reactions are generally disproportionate to the offense. Very often they haven't cried in years. Or like me, they've vowed never to become like the person who hurt them. But these types of vows don't heal or fix anything—they only cut us off from our emotions. The man who hasn't cried in thirty years isn't above emotion; he's zeroed them all out. He's detached himself from feeling anything. They usually aren't even aware of their behavior.

My childhood taught me that I couldn't trust anyone. I believed the world was an unfriendly place, which kept me from taking risks, especially where people were concerned. I was trying to protect myself, but all I did was bottle up the rage and limit my joy. I needed the Spirit to renew my thinking and restore my emotions. I needed him to show me how to rebuild the broken places. But before all that, I needed to answer a simple question: *Do I want to be healed?*

Do you?

- If the answer is yes, I dare you to be brave and recall the moment that was so painful to you. Visualize yourself in the situation. Do you see Jesus? If you don't see him, keep looking around the room until you find him. Where is he? What is he doing? What's his manner like? Pay close attention to the details. Does he want you to come to him? Can you move toward him? Now that you've moved toward him, what's happening? What is he doing? How do you feel?

- There is something powerful that happens when we can see Jesus with us even in the midst of a terrible situation. Knowing that he was there, that he's always been there, waiting for you to come to him. If you were able to move through the previous guided prayer, I'll now ask you if you're ready to forgive and let it go. If yes, speak those words of forgiveness out loud and find the freedom you've been looking for.

- If you're not sure where to begin, I encourage you to ask the Holy Spirit. "Are there any places where I'm holding onto unforgiveness, or not receiving your grace? Please reveal them to me." Then move through the guided prayer above.

- Finally, if you're aware that you're using external vices to cope with uncomfortable emotions, you already know there is something wrong. Those things (television, drugs, alcohol, smoking, social media, sex, or something else) will never comfort you. They will never fill you up. Ask the Holy Spirit to bring to the surface the root cause of the problem, the things that are hurting your heart. Then move through the guided prayers above.

"We now have this light shining in our hearts, but we ourselves are like fragile clay jars containing this great treasure. This makes it clear that our great power is from God, not from ourselves."[12]

CHAPTER 7

HEALING & RESTORATION

"Here we are," Colin said pulling into a narrow driveway.

My stomach had been in knots ever since we landed in England a few days earlier. My older brother Colin and Connie chatted easily on the drive, catching up on family and work. But I was extremely uncomfortable. *Why did I need to forgive Ron?* He was a monster! He'd made my childhood a scary and vulnerable place to be. I inherited his brokenness and struggled through multiple marriages as a result.

I'd been battling through unforgiveness and bitterness ever since Ruby first suggested I forgive him. I was still wrestling with my decision when Colin pulled into the driveway. He'd agreed to arrange a meeting for us when I next visited England as both he and my younger brother Michael were still in contact with Ron. Colin switched off the engine and opened the door, while I glanced out the window.

A little old man walked out of the house toward us. *Was that Ron?* My mind was racing. He was smaller than I remembered, with white hair and rosy cheeks; he certainly didn't look like the ogre who'd terrorized my childhood. I slowly got out of the car, while Colin reached out to Ron. I cautiously followed, awkwardly embracing Ron before introducing myself and Connie to his wife, Maxine.

Maxine led us inside. A sort of nervous chatter followed as Colin and the women filled in the details of the past twenty years while Ron and I sat and listened. I can only imagine how uneasy his wife was. After a while, the tension broke and I realized it was time for me to speak. I wish I could remember what I said, or how I brought it up, but it's all a blur to me now. I only remember that I spoke forgiveness to Ron, and in the next moment, we were both expressing how very sorry we were. With tears in our eyes, we embraced again—reconciled, and to some degree, restored.

I never saw Ron again. Sometime later his wife sent me a letter. She thanked me for coming and told me that my coming had also sweetened her relationship with Ron, and his relationship with their family. My forgiving Ron had changed her life. The freedom and release I experienced as a result of forgiving Ron had changed my life too. How thankful I was for the sweet healing waters of the Holy Spirit, and for Ruby, who responded to his gentle presence and encouraged me to do what I hadn't wanted to face.

AMBASSADORS OF RECONCILIATION

Our sin and brokenness affect not only ourselves, but our relationships, trickling down through generations, friends, and everyone we touch. It sweeps through families and communities like a contagion, which is why in the Bible, our sin is often likened to leprosy.

Leprosy is a highly contagious disease. In the days of Jesus, those infected were forced to stay away from their families, and often lived outside of town in caves and other self-made camps. When they did travel, they were required to yell, "Unclean! Unclean!" to protect those nearby who might come into contact with them. Lepers were not able to worship in the temple. There was no cure. Touching another human almost certainly meant infecting them and passing on their disease. And it was painful. Leprosy damaged the nerves, leading to swelling, numbness, and disfiguration.

In the days of Jesus, there was no known cure other than a miraculous healing. Much like sin, leprosy affected a person's entire life. And so, when I see Jesus, filled with pity, touch a man with leprosy—knowing that Jesus would be unclean from this interaction and could become leprous himself—I am moved. There are a number of stories where Jesus cures a leper; the gospel of Mark tells my favorite one.

"If you will," a leprous man implored Jesus, "you can make me clean." And Jesus responded, "'I will; be clean.' And immediately the leprosy left him, and he was made clean."[1] This man wasn't just set free from his leprosy—he was restored to his community. To his family. To God. He had been healed physically, emotionally, relationally, and spiritually.

Then Jesus charged this man to show himself to the priest as proof of his healing (the priest was in charge of reentry into the temple and society) and bring an offering for his cleansing. He additionally told the man not to tell anyone on the way. "But," Mark tells us, the man "went out and began to talk freely about it, and to spread the news."[2] His healing had not only changed his life, but as he returned to his family and to his community, his return as a whole man would change their lives too. He had to tell people about it. He was not the same.

In 2 Corinthians 5:17, we learn that when we are *in* Christ—when we receive the sacrifice of Jesus' life as the payment for our sins—we become a new creation. "The old has passed away; behold, the new has come." We too were stuck in broken relationships we couldn't fix. We too were separated from God because of our sin. We too were struggling through the crippling emotional effects of living in a fallen world. But now the new has come. We are a new creation.

Paul goes on to say that this is a gift from God, who has reconciled us to himself through Jesus, "and gave us the ministry of reconciliation."[3] God reconciled us to himself, not counting our sins against us, and now he has given us that same ministry of reconciliation. "Therefore, we are ambassadors for Christ, God making his appeal through us. We implore you on behalf of Christ, be reconciled to God."[4] It's not just for us, but for others.

LIVING WATER

On the last day of the Feast of Tabernacles, Jesus stood up at the temple and said, "If anyone thirsts, let him come to me and drink. Whoever believes in me, as the Scripture has said, 'Out of his heart will flow rivers of living water.'"[5] As part of the ceremony on the last day of the feast, the priests would draw water from the Pool of Siloam and pour it over the altar. John gives us a little more insight: Jesus was talking about the Holy Spirit who would be given to those who believe.

To the woman at the well, Jesus said, "Everyone who drinks of this water will be thirsty again, but whoever drinks of the water that I will give him will never be thirsty again. The water that I will give him will become in him a spring of water welling up to eternal life."[6] The living water that Jesus gives—the Holy Spirit—becomes a living spring of water within you, overflowing and touching every area of your life.

There is a healing that comes like living water when we choose to forgive those who have wronged us. The healing comes to us, and also through us. "God's love," Paul wrote, "has been poured into our hearts through the Holy Spirit who has been given to us."[7] I didn't know when I spoke to Ron that it would affect countless others in his family. The effects of sin and brokenness are so far reaching. But the healing water of the Holy Spirit reaches even further.

It reminds me of when God called Moses to speak to the rock in the desert. "Take the staff, and assemble the congregation, you and Aaron your brother, and tell the rock before their eyes to yield its water. So you shall bring water out of the rock for them and give drink to the congregation and their cattle."[8] There is an element of faith required. Trust requires risk, but it is so very worth it. Just like the water poured over the altar, touching everything in its path, the Holy Spirit will flow out of your life touching everyone you meet.

THE HOLY SPIRIT RESTORES WHAT WAS LOST

On another trip to England, I drove to the location of my earliest childhood memory in Kingston. I was not quite four years old, but I can vividly remember a large group of people silhouetted against a huge bonfire in the middle of a crossroads. They were dancing, running, jumping, and celebrating right in the middle of the street. It was Victory Day. World War II was over. I remember it being a time of great joy; my mother has since reminded me that most of the people were probably drunk.

I pulled up to the junction of St. George's Road and Elm Road where I spent my earlier years. Our home—177 Elm Road—stood at the end of a terrace of four houses. It was smaller than I remembered, and older too. Built sometime in the 1890s, the bricks had a yellow, almost ochre-colored tint from the local clay, a familiar feature in the bricks of London. We lived in the home up until the bombing raids, and my mother brought Colin and me back after the damages to the home had been fixed from the bombings.

As I looked around, the memories still came rushing in: the tiny front yard, no more than eight feet deep from the sidewalk to the house where Colin used to store his motorcycle, the black coal hole plate near the front door, the white steps my mother took great pride in shining, and the familiar Alexandra Pub across the street—my second home as a teenager.*

It was nearing lunchtime, so I headed into the Alexandra for a quick bite.

"Do you know if anyone in the neighborhood is still around from the war days?" I asked the barman. "Maybe the Huson's, or the Strutt family?"

I hadn't planned on meeting up with old neighbors, but after seeing our old home, I was feeling nostalgic.

---

* Coal was delivered through that hole from the street. The hole led to the basement coal cellar.

"Yeah," he said slowly, "I think I've heard of them."

We talked a bit more and I learned that he was relatively new to the area; he wouldn't be able to provide any real connections for me to follow up on. I told him about playing in the bomb crater playground with my friends—now a construction site for the new buildings in the neighborhood. He was too young to remember much from that era, so after a while I stopped talking and got on with my lunch. A few minutes later, someone tapped me on the shoulder.

"I overheard your conversation," an elderly man said as I turned around to face him. "You won't remember me," he went on, "but during the air raids, I used to help your mom. I would carry you down into the air-raid shelter at night. You were just a baby."

I was completely blown away. He introduced himself as Jack Fry, and we spent the next hour talking as he told me more about what those years had been like, including his own experiences in the war. Jack had lived three houses up from our home at the other end of the terrace and was one of the last survivors from the war some fifty years earlier.

The death of my father in the war before I was born has always been a great loss in my life. I never got to touch the bristles on his cheek. Never got to smell his aftershave or watch him love my mother. But talking with Jack, and learning that someone had been there, carrying me and keeping me safe when my father couldn't, touched a deep wound in me. I had forgiven and allowed the Holy Spirit to touch Ron through me, and now I was being touched by the Holy Spirit myself. God my Father had been looking out for me, protecting me, and loving me long before I knew him.

Sometime later, I told my mother about meeting Jack and the conversation we shared. I'd never known of Jack's existence. I hadn't recalled my mother ever talking about him.

"Do you remember him?" I asked.

"Oh yes," she said. "I remember him well. Most everyone had lost someone in the war, and with the bombings in our community, life was very difficult. I'm so thankful for Jack and all of the others who reached out to help us in the midst of their own difficulties!"

I was too young to understand or remember much from those days, but after learning of Jack's existence, and after forgiving Ron, I felt something like the living waters of the Holy Spirit bubbling up inside of me. The once leaky and broken conduits were flowing with life once again. Healing is not usually a one-step process, but forgiveness is always a good place to start.

REFLECTION & PRAYER

I think part of the reason why I love the story of the leprous man is because I see so much of myself in him. I was born with a severe case of clubfoot, a physical deformity that affected most of my childhood. While my mother sought various treatments, I wore leg irons that reached from my foot all the way to a padded belt that surrounded my waist. For a time, I had daily physical therapy at the hospital, but the treatments were all found to be ineffective. Some of the treatments involved me being left at the hospital without my family, which felt like abandonment at the time.

I was teased mercilessly for years. I can remember being so angry, I pulled off one of my irons and chased a child around the schoolyard intending to hurt him with it, the way his words had hurt me. But the torment wasn't just at school. One of my aunts would tease me relentlessly, calling me Little Cripple Bobby, and even sang a song to provoke me.* One day my mother found me outside; I had thrown myself onto the rubbish pile. I thought I was worthless. I was isolated, angry, and broken.

When I was eleven, we met a young doctor who was willing to try a new experimental surgery on my leg. It would involve breaking my left ankle and restructuring the bones in such a way that lengthened the leg to be equal to that of my right. They would then place an insert in my

---

* Here's the song she used to sing, "Bobby Shafto's gone to sea / with silver buckles on his knees / when he comes home, he'll marry me / Bobby, Bobby Shafto." My braces had silver buckles. Why she was so determined to hurt and provoke me, I can't say.

Achilles tendon to accommodate for the new length of my leg. The pain following the surgery was excruciating, but the restructuring was a success, and I was eventually able to run and play just like the other kids.*

After the surgery, my life changed drastically. I was able to participate in team sports—something I only ever dreamed of doing—and compete in individual sports! The surgery hadn't just affected me physically, but like the leper, it affected me emotionally and relationally too. Looking back, I can see that I wasn't just physically crippled, but emotionally and spiritually crippled too. My childhood had been so dark, and this physical healing had allowed the light to start trickling in.

Our outward conditions, emotional deficiencies, and past traumas often have a greater impact on our lives than we realize. Learning to forgive, opening our hearts to receive healing after disappointment, and allowing the Holy Spirit to touch every area of our lives will touch more people than just you.

- Is there someone you need to forgive?
- Ask the Holy Spirit to reveal any areas in your life where your heart has been hardened or calloused by a lack of forgiveness. Remember, the Holy Spirit does not condemn, he convicts. He speaks truth and brings light to dark places.
- If the Holy Spirit has revealed a person you need to forgive, or an area where you need to seek forgiveness, confess that to him now. Ask the Holy Spirit to help you forgive if you feel you're not yet ready. Ask him to soften your heart.
- Follow the Holy Spirit's leading and speak forgiveness. Be a conduit of blessing and living water to the spiritually thirsty around you.

---

* It turns out, I was the first boy to have the procedure done in Europe, and quite possibly the world!

CHAPTER 8

BEARING SPIRITUAL FRUIT

Forgiving Ron opened me up to the Spirit in new ways. Connie and I became more involved with Pastor Larry Eddings and the Wind of the Spirit Ministries, where we received teachings on the Holy Spirit, spiritual gifts, healing, sexual brokenness, and deliverance. Pastor Larry's goal was always to equip the saints for ministry, and we began to see this taking place in our own lives. The Spirit was moving —not just at church and in ministry—but with our neighbors, co-workers, and others who didn't yet know Jesus. Connie and I became part of the support team for Wind of the Spirit events, and eventually, I was asked to join the teaching team.

I was still working in Seattle as a creative designer and had developed a friendship with Ruth, a saleswoman I often worked with. Ruth was Jewish, liberal, and a lesbian, but her partner was English, so we had an area of commonality. Despite our differences, Ruth and I talked about our faith often. She believed that we all worshipped the same God but were on different paths to being with him. I shared the gospel with her many times, and even though we disagreed, we were able to continue our friendship and talk about spiritual things.

During one of our discussions, I shared with Ruth how important forgiveness is—a core element of the Christian faith—and how necessary it had been for me to forgive my stepfather Ron for his abusive behavior toward me as a child. As she listened, her face hardened and her entire demeanor changed. Clearly, it triggered something in her, but she said nothing about it. On our way to a presentation appointment not long after, she opened up to me.

"There's something I want you to know . . . " She'd been quiet for most of the drive, and her words came slowly. "My dad abused me as teenager." She exhaled shakily. "I had two abortions before I was sixteen. They were both his . . ."

We'd just arrived at our appointment, so there was no time to respond or discuss. I nodded at her in silent acknowledgement, and we got out of the car. What a weight she'd been carrying!

"Thank you for sharing your story with me." I said as soon as we were back in the car, silently praying that the Holy Spirit would give me words to comfort and guide her.

Ruth nodded. I wanted to leave it at that, but I felt a strong prompting from the Holy Spirit to revisit our previous conversation about forgiveness. I took a deep breath.

"Do you remember when I talked to you about forgiving my stepfather?"

She nodded.

"I think you might need to forgive your dad . . . "

Ruth's whole body hardened as she vehemently shook her head in disagreement.

". . . for your own sake, Ruth. Not because he deserves it."

She continued shaking her head. She could not and would not forgive him. The conversation was over. It hadn't gone the way I hoped, but I left it at that. I had been obedient.

A few weeks went by, and I responded to the Spirit's prompting again. "Ruth, is your dad still alive?"

"Yes," she said hesitantly, "he lives in New York, but I haven't seen him for twenty years . . ." her voice trailed off.

"Wouldn't it be wonderful if you could find a way to forgive him and let go of the weight you've been carrying?"

"I . . . I can't do that," she said shaking her head again, and then more resolutely, "I won't do that."

The conversation was over, but Ruth was still open to talking about forgiveness. From time to time over the next few weeks she would ask questions and we'd discuss what forgiveness is, what it isn't, and why it's so important.

Then one day she surprised me. "I bought a ticket to New York," she said nervously, "I'm going to see my mom and dad. I'm scared, but I think I need to do it."

Ruth did forgive her dad, and they were—to some extent—reconciled. Sadly, her mother refused to believe that anything Ruth had told her was true. She wouldn't hear it. Ruth accepted that she would not be able to reconcile with her mother, but even so, she later told me what a heavy burden had been lifted in forgiving her parents and letting go of the bitterness.

THE FRUIT OF THE SPIRIT

When we walk daily with the Holy Spirit—talking with him, listening to him, and following his lead—our lives will begin to bear good fruit, also known as the fruit of the Spirit: love, joy, peace, patience, kindness, goodness, faithfulness, gentleness, and self-control. Unfortunately, many believers have grown up believing that the fruit of the Spirit are attributes or values, rather than a natural byproduct of walking in the Spirit. But we can't produce spiritual fruit on our own. We can't work harder to be patient, or more joy-filled, just as plants can't work harder to produce fruit and flowers.

"I have been crucified with Christ," Paul wrote in Galatians. "It is no longer I who live, but Christ who lives in me. And the life I now live in the flesh I live by faith in the Son of God, who loved me and gave himself for me."[1] We live our lives by faith, not in the strength of our flesh. In other words, don't think you can live the spirit-filled life doing the same things you've always done. It won't work. This is what Timothy called people who have the *appearance* of godliness, but deny God's power.[2]

Jesus warned his followers about these kinds of false prophets or religious imposters; they were people with the outward appearance of goodness, but devoid of spiritual fruit. "You will recognize them by their fruits," Jesus said. The fruit is the evidence of the tree's health. The overflow of our inner lives reveals our spiritual health, whether our actions are spirit-filled, or just empty religious works. "Are grapes gathered from thornbushes, or figs from thistles? So, every healthy tree bears good fruit, but the diseased tree bears bad fruit."[3]

Jesus saved us not because of our righteous works or good deeds, "but because of his mercy. He saved us through the washing of rebirth and renewal by the Holy Spirit."[4] As our minds are daily renewed and washed by the Holy Spirit, our lives will naturally produce spiritual fruit. We don't need to perform, spiritually speaking. When we are born again, our spirit is transformed, but our minds need to continually be renewed.

The nine spiritual fruits listed in Galatians are not an exhaustive list of what the Holy Spirit produces, but evidence of his presence in a believer's life. Apart from the Spirit, we won't produce anything of value. Jesus said, "I am the vine; you are the branches. Whoever abides in me and I in him, he it is that bears much fruit, for apart from me you can do nothing."[5]

DIVINE APPOINTMENTS IN THE SPIRIT

Sharing with Ruth had been a risky experiment. I don't know if she ever became a believer, but I do know the Holy Spirit was working in her life. I was still young in my faith and apprehensive about sharing, but Ruth's story encouraged me. I was grateful to be a part of her healing journey and wanted to be used by the Spirit to heal others.

Our neighbor Chuck had been diagnosed with cancer and would very likely die from the disease. I began to pray that the Holy Spirit would give me the courage to share with him, and perhaps be part of his healing. I was so nervous about sharing that every time I pulled into our carport at home, I would begin praying before I got out of the car, just in case I saw him. One day, as I was sitting in my car praying, I was startled by a voice outside.

"Hello." Chuck smiled at me through the car window.

"How are you doing?" I asked, both surprised to see him and nervous. This was the moment I'd been praying for. Chuck gave me a brief update on his prognosis, which wasn't good.

I wasn't sure what else to say, so I asked, "Can I pray with you?"

Chuck's entire face lit up. "Yes!" He seemed eager and expectant in a way that surprised me.

I don't remember what I prayed, but after I finished, I invited him to our Monday night small group at Jack and Ruby's house. Chuck knew Jack from the shipyard and said he'd like to join us. I made plans to pick him up and take him with me to the meeting.

Chuck was warmly welcomed at the group. Within a few minutes he was chatting with Jack about work. Moments later, Ruby interrupted.

"Have you ever accepted Jesus as your Lord and Savior?" she asked Chuck.

"No, I haven't."

"We should do that right now," Ruby said, and began leading him in a prayer of saving grace. I was amazed how easily it happened and so thankful that Chuck now had the assurance of eternal life. Within a few months he passed away. How thankful I was that I'd not let my nervousness get in the way of Chuck's spiritual healing!

I was working from home as a freelance designer, but I wasn't very successful. I wondered if I might do better in a group setting, perhaps in an exhibit designer position like I'd had in England. Connie and I began praying for God's will for my work, when I received two unsolicited phone calls from the owners of two different companies. Both offers were from companies based in Portland, Oregon looking to set up offices in Seattle, and both needed an experienced designer to complete their team. The job descriptions and benefits were identical, and each company wanted to hire me.

Connie and I knew the Lord had brought both of these offers, but we had no idea which one to choose. I met with the owners and liked each of them. After a few weeks of deliberation, one of the owners called to say that he couldn't wait any longer—he needed my answer by Monday. We shared our dilemma with the pastor at our church. That Sunday evening, the pastor prayed, "Lord, we know that Bob is a gifted artist and he can *draw*. But we are in a *drawn* situation and ask for your Holy Spirit's guidance."

After a brief pause, one of the other prayer warriors in attendance spoke up. "When the disciples were looking to replace Judas, they *drew* lots, and as a result chose Matthias."

And that was it. I had my answer—I would call the owner named Matthias on Monday morning and accept the position!

I enjoyed working with a team of people again as a creative designer. The company grew, and over time, so did my workload. Most of my days were spent in meetings and presentations, leaving the design work for the early morning and late evening hours. The long commute only added to the stress. Missed ferries and the additional seventy miles of driving were exhausting. Eventually it became too much, and I told my boss I was going to resign.

There were now two owners at my company and neither of them wanted me to leave. They proposed that I would make a good salesman, which I thought was a terrible idea. Salespeople always seemed pushy and self-centered to me, but they made a good case, sharing the qualities I had that made them think it might be a good fit. I was a good listener, had an analytical mind, and was solution oriented. Plus, the position would be more flexible time-wise and they would start me on a sliding salary. Connie and I prayed and felt the Holy Spirit saying yes, so we agreed.

My new boss had an aggressive style and personality, but she was a good teacher, and I learned a lot from her. Every day I asked God for victory in the marketplace and began to build up a good client base. I found that helping clients make good marketing presentations felt more like consulting than selling, which was very rewarding for me. I was also praying for my boss, Barbara. She could be difficult, and at times, somewhat abusive to her team.

"It seems like you don't know if I'm your mother, your sister, or your daughter!" She blurted out in frustration one day. "You must have a problem with the fact that your boss is a woman!"

I was dumbfounded. I had no difficulty with her being a woman. I turned my morning commute into my prayer time. "Lord, please show me how to work with Barbara. She knows I'm a Christian and it seems like her real problem with me is you. I need your help."

But I wasn't the only one experiencing problems with her. One day a fellow saleswoman was so fed up, she yelled at Barbara right in the middle of the office. Our office had an open floor plan, so not only did everyone hear the confrontation, we all felt as if we were a part of it. Barbara stormed out. Several hours later, I received a call asking if my co-worker Eli and I would come speak with her at her home.

She was visibly upset and in tears, but wanted to know the truth—was she really as bad as the saleswoman had made her seem? I asked the Holy Spirit for guidance, and when I spoke, told her the truth in the gentlest way possible. She thanked us both for coming and for our honesty. Eli and I went back to the office and quietly returned to our work, while I wondered about the earlier events of the day. *Was the Holy Spirit working on Barbara? Had he used me to help her see herself, and perhaps him more clearly?*

During one of our sales meetings, we were instructed to choose prospective clients from leads they had collected at a recent trade show. Barbara spread a stack of business cards out on the table. After everyone else had chosen, I took the card for the Discovery Channel as no one else wanted it. I set up a meeting with them and we hit it off immediately. My contact Gil was married to an English woman from south London where I'd gone to art school. He invited us to submit a proposal which was later accepted.

Our first pre-show exhibit setup with Discovery was in Portland, Oregon. Gil flew out from the East Coast to meet us and stayed with his mother. He and his team were pleased with our work, and our relationship began to grow. Our time difference was not a strain, but instead gave us an extra six hours to work on projects each day (when their team was finished for the day, they would pass the project on to our team to finish). One success led to another, and we were soon asked to partner with them on all their projects. As their company grew and launched new TV channels, my skills and experience grew as well.

Even in these small business dealings, I saw the Spirit of God leading me and granting me favor. My relationship with Gil grew easily because his wife and I were both English, his mother lived in the northwest, and I always dealt honestly and fairly with his company. Once, when our team mistakenly installed an exhibit booth facing the wrong direction, I feared all would be lost. But after we quickly corrected the problem, they told us how impressed they were with how we handled the situation. As a result of being in a sales position and having a very successful working relationship with Discovery, I was also financially rewarded. It's amazing to me how the Lord tied all of these details together. His provision is always perfect.

Sometime later, Barbara and I traveled together to New York for a meeting with the Discovery Channel to review our partnership. Our hotel was across the street from Saint Patrick's Cathedral, which I'd always wanted to see, so after the meeting I asked if she'd like to join me. We both sat quietly on the pews admiring the incredible architecture and atmosphere of the building. Suddenly it struck me that the Holy Spirit had led us both into a house of worship. *Wow, God*, I thought. *I came in to see the architecture, but perhaps you had something else in mind for Barbara.* And so, as we sat together in silence, I spent nearly twenty minutes praying for Barbara and asking the Spirit to speak to her. I believed in faith he was.

Shortly after that trip, Barbara was fired. I have no idea what the Spirit was doing that day, but I'm grateful he gave me the opportunity to pray for her and bring her into his house of worship.

REFLECTION & PRAYER

We don't always know how or when the Holy Spirit will use us. All we can do is stay connected to Jesus and allow the Holy Spirit to bring forth his spiritual fruit in our lives. As we move into the next section, we'll talk more about manifestations of the Spirit, of which I've been blessed to see many times in my life. I share these stories as a testimony of the daily abiding presence of the Holy Spirit and his work in my life. They are evidence that he can work in anyone and at any time, and that we do not have to wait for large events or assemblies to see the Spirit move. He invites us to watch him work as he daily produces fruit in our lives.

- What fruit have you seen the Spirit produce in your life? How do you know it's of him?
- Take a moment to reflect on how the Spirit has led you to where you are today (whether you were aware of it or not). Make special note of the times you were not aware of his movement or presence until afterwards. Now apply those insights to the situations you're currently in. How might the Spirit be moving in ways of which you were unaware?
- Where do you spend most of your time each day? With whom? Who might the Spirit be leading you to pray for, or encourage, or minister to? This might be your place of business, community groups, children and their teachers, etc.
- Ask the Holy Spirit to open your eyes to how he's moving in your life right now. Ask him to show you how to pray not only for your situation, but for those he wants you to notice.

CHAPTER 9

PRAYING IN THE SPIRIT

"**D**o you have a little brown dog?"

It was a strange question to ask someone you didn't know, but that was part of the assignment. We'd been placed in small groups during a Wind of the Spirit Healing Seminar and challenged to ask the Holy Spirit to reveal painful areas where he wanted us to be set free. One by one, we shared our struggle, and then the group would pray. We were praying for a man in his early sixties who'd been married five or six times. He knew he was experiencing emotional difficulties; he couldn't remember the last time he'd cried.

". . . or have you ever owned a little brown dog?" I asked again, feeling somewhat silly.

We'd begun as we always did, asking the Holy Spirit to show us how to pray. But as we waited, I kept seeing a short-haired brown dog running back and forth in my mind. I didn't know if it was a vision, a sign, or if it meant anything at all. The man looked at me quizzically, clearly uncomfortable with the question, but said nothing. The group opened their eyes slightly, peering around in the awkward silence.

"Yes, I did have a little brown dog," he finally answered before quickly adding, "but I don't want to talk about it!"

I was as surprised as everyone else. The group encouraged him not to ignore this prompting of the Holy Spirit and gently urged him to let the Spirit guide him through this memory of his dog. After some initial reluctance, he agreed to share his story.

"I was about ten years old," he began, "and I was very rebellious. Especially toward my dad. Stubborn, too. I refused to listen to anything he said. Every time my dad asked me to do something, I would disobey, until one day . . . he hit me." He paused for a moment. "And he warned me, he said, 'If you keep this up, the punishments are going to get worse and worse!' But I didn't listen." He grimaced.

"Well, one day . . . I don't know what I did . . . something I wasn't supposed to do. My dad grabbed me and my dog and took us both to the barn. He was just a little thing, but my dad threw a rope over the beam and tied a noose around my dog's neck! I just watched him do it. I watched him kill my dog."

"Then my dad said, 'Now perhaps you'll listen up when I tell you not to do something.' I was terrified he'd do something even worse to me, so I ran and hid."

A few people in the group had tears in their eyes, but the man didn't cry; his gaze was fixed on the ground in front of him.

"That's terrible," someone in the group said softly, while the rest of the group murmured in agreement. "How painful that must have been for you. But you need to forgive him to be free."

"No," he insisted. "I can't do it."

The group continued to encourage him. Eventually, guided by the Holy Spirit and through clenched teeth, he spoke forgiveness to his dad. In an instant, tears filled his eyes and he began to weep. We wept with him, praising God for the healing that he received; he was set free from the bondage of the past fifty years.

It's one thing to hope and believe for yourself, but quite another to take a risk and trust the Holy Spirit for someone else. But that is why the gifts were given—to be a part of the Spirit's healing ministry for others. Through the group's willingness to pray; my willingness to look foolish asking about a little brown dog; and the man's willingness to be vulnerable and forgive, we witnessed an incredible manifestation of the Spirit that no doubt changed the man's life.

MANIFESTATIONS OF THE SPIRIT

I find that while most believers desire to see the Spirit move in the lives of others, bringing healing, restoration, and hope, they are desperately afraid of what it might look like for the Spirit to use them. They are afraid of looking foolish or losing control. They are afraid they will make a mistake. They wonder if their gifts would be better given to the pastor or someone else who knows more than they do.

Perhaps this is why we see less of the Spirit moving in our churches today: we are waiting for our pastors to make room for the Spirit, rather than being available to be used by the Spirit ourselves.

In 1 Corinthians 12:7, Paul tell us that, "**To each** is given the manifestation of the Spirit for the common good" (emphasis mine). These *manifestations* are the visible signs of the Spirit's work in your life. In other words, you've each been given a spiritual gift—evidence of the Holy Spirit's work in your life—so that you can help one another.

> For to one is given through the Spirit the utterance of wisdom, and to another the utterance of knowledge according to the same Spirit, to another faith by the same Spirit, to another gifts of healing by the one Spirit, to another the working of miracles, to another prophecy, to another the ability to distinguish between spirits, to another various kinds of tongues, to another the interpretation of tongues. All these are empowered by one and the same Spirit, who apportions to each one individually as he wills.[1]

In short, the manifestations of the Spirit are wisdom, word of knowledge, faith, healing, miracles, prophecy, discernment, speaking in tongues, and the interpretation of tongues. Paul spends nearly three chapters discussing these spiritual gifts in 1 Corinthians 12–14, perhaps because these are for all of us. There is one Spirit, Paul writes just before this passage, but he moves in different ways. Scripture provides a template for how the Spirit moves and works, but you won't really know until you experience him moving and working in and through you.

These manifestations of the Spirit are not to be confused with the additional gifts the Spirit gives us for service as described in Romans 12, and the ministerial gifts given to equip the saints listed in Ephesians 4. I would argue that for the church's benefit, the Spirit gives the gifts needed for the assignment, and perhaps for a one-time, single use only. It may be more than one gift!

When I saw the image of the little brown dog, I wasn't sure if the Spirit was giving me a word, an image of knowledge, or a vision. You could argue that I was using the gift of service and had a word of knowledge. But I didn't know what was happening. It was an entirely new experience for me. I had to trust that the Spirit was leading me, and if not, that he was able to redirect us.

Sometimes, holding too tightly to rigid definitions and understandings can prevent us from participating in what the Spirit is doing. I was simply praying for a man who knew he needed emotional healing. As I did, I saw a little brown dog. *Was it something I ate that morning? My mind running wild?* I wouldn't know unless I asked. As it turned out, the Spirit had given us the key to unlocking this man's brokenness through the image of a little brown dog.

There are still moments in prayer where I'm unsure; there is a risk to walking with the Holy Spirit. You always need to have complete dependency on him. You don't need to know all the details for the Spirit to use you; in fact, you usually don't. It's not about you—it's about the Holy Spirit ministering through you. I like to remind myself that the Holy Spirit is more than able to correct any mistake or misunderstanding I may have in prayer.

Trusting the Voice of God

Before I moved to the States, I traveled all over the world working as a creative designer for the British government. I had fond memories of traveling to the Philippines, and so when the Wind of the Spirit healing team said they were traveling to Manila, I was excited to join them. I remember wanting to help the Filipino people I met on my travels, some of whom worked on benches all day, and then slept under those same benches each night. In an effort to give back to the people, I arranged for a shipment of products they were making to be sent to the UK for resale, but I'm not sure it made much of a difference.

When the need is so great, and the culture is so different, it's hard to know *how* to help. A Swiss man I met on the plane told me he'd given cash to a family to help fix their leaky roof, install flooring, and buy shoes for their kids. When he visited a year later, he realized they'd used the money to purchase a TV and a drink cabinet. When he asked them about it, they explained that the roof had always leaked, everyone had mud floors, and their children had never owned shoes, so they'd be okay. Now they had more wonderful things.

To have the opportunity to go back to the Philippines as a believer meant that I had something even more lasting and wonderful than a TV to offer. Something that truly would change their lives within their culture, rather than trying to change their lives according to my culture. My role on this trip was as a prayer support partner under the leadership of Larry and Audrey Eddings.

We arrived in Manila on a Saturday and everyone who was to be involved in the next couple of weeks gathered in a restaurant for dinner that night. After introductions and formalities, the local bishop announced the Sunday morning speaking engagements for the team members who would be going to several different churches in the Manila area.

"Bob Cashmore, . . ." the bishop called in a loud voice. I looked up from my dinner. I hadn't expected to hear my name called. "You'll be speaking at Church by the Highway in Bacoor, Cavite. Your prayer partner, Miss Anne Key, will be traveling with you."

What? Had they made a mistake? I wasn't on the teaching team! I went to bed that evening and wrestled all night over what I'd say. What did the Holy Spirit want me to say? I wouldn't have considered myself a teacher, in fact, I still don't. But I knew I'd need the gift of teaching if the Spirit was going to use me. I prayed for that, too. In the early hours of the morning, a Scripture came into my mind—Luke 4:18–19.

> The Spirit of the Lord is upon me, because he has anointed me to proclaim good news to the poor. He has sent me to proclaim liberty to the captives and recovering of sight to the blind, to set at liberty those who are oppressed, to proclaim the year of the Lord's favor.

The next morning, I stood up in Bacoor and shared from my heart on the Scripture the Spirit had given me the night before. I trusted that whatever the Spirit wanted to say would be given to me at the appropriate time. More and more people came in as I shared (mostly women and children), and I was amazed to see that as I finished speaking, the place was filled. Miss Anne, who'd been praying the whole time, motioned that I should give an altar call.

"For the men to come forward for prayer," she whispered.

I hadn't seen many men, but heeded her suggestion anyway. "I'd like to invite the men forward to receive prayer."

Men seemed to come out of nowhere, as if the structure of the building was alive. Many of them confessed their struggles with sexual purity, and through prayer that morning were set free. Over the next twelve years, I made five more trips to the Philippines with Wind of the Spirit Ministries. Each time, I saw the Holy Spirit use me in unique ways and I saw him manifest his gifts and power in different ways. I have loved every experience and opportunity with him I've been given, but each time, I have been challenged in my faith to trust him.

During one of our trips, a young boy ran up and handed me a picture he'd drawn. The picture was of a man wearing a camouflage uniform, holding a gun.

"You," he said, pointing at the picture and then pointing again at me.

His English was limited, but after a short explanation I realized he had drawn a picture of me fighting in spiritual warfare. I thanked him and put the picture in my pocket. I didn't think much of it until we returned to Florida and I shared about our trip to the Philippines with the church there. As I was speaking, a few small children sat on the floor in the front of the sanctuary drawing. The church encouraged their participation in the service, believing that the Spirit might lead or inspire their creativity. When I'd finished talking, one of the boys ran up to me with a picture.

"This is you," he said.

The picture he'd drawn was nearly identical to the one from the young boy in the Philippines. I'd saved the other picture, but it hadn't struck me as significant until I realized the Holy Spirit was ministering to me through the artwork. I was stunned. I hadn't mentioned the drawing during my talk. It's a reminder that we often don't see the spiritual battles we are engaging in, just like we often miss seeing the spiritual gifts and callings in ourselves. How faithful the Spirit is to encourage and prompt us to step into the callings we have received.

LET US USE OUR GIFTS

"If you have a testimony from our time together that you'd like to share, please come forward."

Pastor Larry stood at the front of the church in Baggio City looking out over the local congregation. We'd had a wonderful time of healing and prayer, and now it was time to close out the conference. One of the local pastors walked up to the front and stood next to Pastor Larry to share his testimony.

"This has been a wonderfully refreshing experience for me," he said. "I'm looking forward to sharing the powerful teachings and demonstration of the Spirit that I've learned and received here with my home church . . ."

At that moment, a noise broke out behind us. I turned around in the front row just in time to see a man staggering down the center aisle toward Pastor Larry. He was frothing at the mouth and making weird screeching noises like I'd never heard before. As the man neared the front of the church, he turned to face the pastor who'd been sharing his testimony. The pastor's face suddenly froze, and he fell to the ground, motionless. The man then turned to face Pastor Larry.

I watched the scene unfold in horror, as if in slow motion. *We need a pastor to remove that man and pray for him!* I thought. As I looked around the room for the person who might handle the situation, Pastor Audrey caught my eye.

"Take that man outside!" she said, as if it was obvious that I was man for the job. Another team member and I jumped to action. Over the rising commotion, we ushered the man outside the main hall while Pastor Larry made his way to the pastor who still lay frozen on the ground. Pastor Larry called for the worship to begin again, and as we exited, we heard him announce that the pastor would continue his testimony to Jesus in heaven. We later learned that he died of a massive heart attack.

Once outside the main hall, Rupert and I began to pray prayers of deliverance with the man. *Holy Spirit*, I prayed, *show us how to pray for this man.*

"Don't let him come back into the fellowship or take communion with us unless you think he is spiritually clean," Pastor Audrey shouted over the singing from inside.

We continued to pray, and as we did, we watched the demonic spirits inhabiting this man be cast out. Although there was no breeze, we noticed the curtains over the window flutter as they left. Eventually, we led the man—now cleansed from any demonic presence and in his right mind—back into the hall where he received Holy Communion.

I'd been looking around for a pastor or someone more experienced or qualified to help this man, but it is the Spirit who qualifies us. We need to use the gifts we've been given, and we need to be open to be given the gifts needed for the situation. I have often felt inadequate, but my weakness doesn't matter, because when I am weak, he is strong.

> Having gifts that differ according to the grace given to us, let us use them: if prophecy, in proportion to our faith; if service, in our serving; the one who teaches, in his teaching; the one who exhorts, in his exhortation; the one who contributes, in generosity; the one who leads, with zeal; the one who does acts of mercy, with cheerfulness. Let love be genuine. Abhor what is evil; hold fast to what is good.[2]

In other words, in his grace God has given us each *different* gifts to do his work. So, if he's given you the ability to prophesy, or serve, or teach—do it with the faith he's given you. Don't hold back! There is a difference between your talents, or natural ability, and a supernatural gift from God. While the Spirit has given you everything you need to use your gift, as is evidenced in Romans 12, it is not you working, but the Holy Spirit working through you.

In Ephesians 4, Paul goes on to talk about the gifts given to equip the saints for the work of the ministry, but he closes this section with an admonition that is for us all: "He makes the whole body fit together perfectly. As each part does its own special work, it helps the other parts grow, so that the whole body is healthy and growing and full of love."[3] We need to use our gifts.

Reflection & Prayer

Years after I became a prayer support partner with Wind of the Spirit Ministries, a friend of ours came to the church for prayer. He loved to swim, and swam laps often, but had misjudged his position in the pool and cracked his head on the concrete during a turn. His head was in pain, and he wasn't able to move his neck. We prayed for him, but nothing happened. He didn't feel anything. A few days later however, as he was driving down the road, he turned to look at the car next to him and realized he could move his neck!

The healing had taken place between the time we prayed with him and his drive in the car. God had completed the healing in his own time, without our presence, because the truth is—he doesn't need us. He invites us to be part of the work he is doing. This takes faith and trust. Faith that the Spirit is guiding you and trust that he is working. You will not always see the final healing, the breakthrough, or the victory, but rest assured the Spirit is still moving.

It is helpful to have others to practice with. During our time with Wind of the Spirit, we would often break into small groups and practice praying for one another, hearing the Spirit for one another, and being a part of bringing healing. We would also pair up with a prayer partner. After times of prayer and ministry, we would debrief with our partners asking what they learned or what they discerned. Our Monday night small group was also a wonderful place to practice and experience our spiritual gifts.

- Read 1 Corinthians 12–14. List the manifestations of the Spirit you see, as well as anything else that stands out to you, like admonitions or exhortations about how to use your spiritual gifts.
- Based on your list above, where do you feel nudged by the Spirit to trust him more?
- What manifestations of the Spirit have you experienced?
- How might you make room for the Spirit as you minister to others?
- Find a prayer partner or a group and commit to regular times of talking with and being open to the Holy Spirit.

Chapter 10

Working Together

Nearly the entire congregation stood at the front of the church before the altar—a large platform about thirty feet long that ran across the width of the room. I looked out over them—now three people deep—feeling completely inadequate for the task at hand. I'd given a talk on the healing power of Jesus that I believed in faith would bring deliverance, but I hadn't expected this. A steady stream of people had flowed to the front since I'd given an invitation to come forward for prayer.

That morning, we'd driven from our hotel through torrential rain to be with the believers at Jesus the Savior United Methodist Church in Bulacan, North Manila. The main roads had flooded, and we'd been forced to take several diversions, but we'd still managed to make it on time. The church was packed. They hadn't come to hear me, but because they were desperate for the work of the Holy Spirit in their lives. They needed healing.

"Holy Spirit," I prayed silently, "please help me. If we're going to get through this, I need you to do your thing."

I knelt down on the platform and began praying for the people who'd come forward, one-by-one, beginning at the right of the stage and slowly making my way across the first row of people. There were prayer requests for physical healing: restored eyesight, hearing, headaches, back pain, and heart problems; and requests for relational healing: reconciliations within families and marriages. There was also a huge need for forgiveness—both of self and others—which led to confession and repentance, and spiritual healing in its own right.

I'd nearly finished with the first row when I noticed a disfigured young man come forward for prayer. He appeared to have physical-control issues and very little control over his arms and legs, which moved in an uncoordinated way. I wasn't sure how to pray for him, or what I expected God to do, so before I reached him, I got up and walked back to the far side of the altar and began praying for the next row.

I continued praying, but stopped again before I reached him. Very often, the Holy Spirit will give me a word of knowledge or some clue as to how to pray for someone, but I'd heard nothing, so I continued skipping over him to pray for others. He was still standing there when I finished praying for the third row, but the Lord hadn't shown me how to pray, so I went back to my seat on the stage and sat down.

The pastor, who was sitting on the stage next to me, caught my attention and motioned in the direction of the young man as if to say, *You're not done praying yet!* Still feeling unsure, I realized that I may not know how to pray, or have a word of knowledge, but I could exercise the gift of faith. I didn't need to know how to pray for the Spirit to move. It was enough to believe the Spirit would touch him in ways beyond my understanding. I made my way back toward the young man, still standing before the platform, and knelt before him. As my eyes met his, I began to weep. Then we hugged for what seemed like a very long time and I told him just how much Jesus loved him.

When I got up, the man smiled and then hobbled back to his family who all came forward to embrace him. Evidently, something had happened. They were aware of it even if I wasn't.

THE BODY OF CHRIST

In the first part of 1 Corinthians 12, Paul provides a list of the nine spiritual gifts we've already discussed. But halfway through the chapter, he shifts gears and begins talking about the body of Christ. Just as there are many parts of the body working together so that you can think and engage with this world, so too there are many parts in the body of Christ. Just like a broken toe causes the entire body to limp, a broken or unused part of the spiritual body causes the whole church to wobble.

Simply put: We need each other. The body isn't able to function properly if we're not using our spiritual gifts. Then Paul provides another partial list of what you might call, church body parts. "And God has appointed in the church first apostles, second prophets, third teachers, then miracles, then gifts of healing, helping, administrating, and various kinds of tongues."[1]

Our tendency is to want to have the most desirable gift. But we can't all be apostles. We aren't all prophets. We don't all have the power to work miracles. The body won't function properly if we're all fighting to be the same part. We not only need to be using our spiritual gifts, but we also need to be working *together*. And so, Paul writes, "you should earnestly desire the most helpful gifts."[2] Rather than desiring the gift we want most, or the one we think is the best or would bring us the most recognition, we should desire the gift that is the most *helpful*.

While I don't consider myself a teacher, I was often called upon to teach when on mission trips in the Philippines. The gift of teaching was needed, and therefore, the most helpful gift in that situation. So, I asked the Spirit to give me the gifts and anointing necessary to do what he had called me to do. The opposite is also true. Sometimes you will have too many teachers and the gift of helps is needed most.

It's easy to think that because we've been used by the Spirit as a teacher in the past, we will always be called upon to be a teacher in the future. We assume we know best how the Spirit can and should use us in the present. But just when you think Paul is finished discussing the spiritual gifts, and just when he's told you to desire the most helpful gifts, he adds, "But now let me show you a way of life that is best of all."[3]

A BETTER WAY

First Corinthians 13 is one of the most quoted Scriptures in the entire Bible—it's all about God's way of love, the better way. But it is rarely understood in the context of spiritual gifts, a conversation Paul is clearly continuing from the previous chapter. Any time you get a large group of people together, you will have challenges. One person wants to do it this way, another wants to do it that way. A group of believers is no different. We each have been given spiritual gifts, we each have a part to play, but above all else, we must choose love.

One afternoon in Manila, we visited a hospital in Quezon City at the request of one of the church deaconesses. Her father was dying, and she wanted me to pray for him. The church pastor and elders decided to join us, and after a long drive we arrived at the hospital—a three-story concrete block building with small windows that overlooked the parking lot. We took the elevator to the third level and entered a large open ward with twenty beds arranged neatly into two rows.

The woman's father looked terrible. He lay on his back, ashen-colored and motionless, hooked up to all sorts of fluids and equipment. She held his hand as our group began to sing praise songs to Jesus. To our surprise, other patients in the ward began to sing with us. At this, her father opened his eyes and looked around. He motioned to speak to his daughter, and I sensed through the Holy Spirit that he was not saved.

"Has your father committed his life to Jesus?" I asked. She translated my question to her father, and he shook his head no. He was not saved.

"I think we should do that now," I said. I was about to pray—which the young woman had requested I do—when the Spirit reminded me that it may be more meaningful if the prayer was spoken in her father's heart language of Tagalog, rather than through translation. I turned to the young pastor next to me.

"Would you like to lead him in a prayer of salvation?"

The young pastor's eyes widened with delight as he turned toward the woman's father. They prayed, and suddenly the room was filled with an air of expectation and joy. God had healed him spiritually—perhaps he would heal him physically as well! The room erupted into song, both patients and nurses singing with us.

Soon, the man was sitting up in bed; the color returned to his face. He looked much better than when we arrived. I realized then that I needed to leave for an evening meeting. As I waited for a cab, I shook hands with the pastor and the elders, and turned to the woman's father to say goodbye. He pulled back the covers and swung his legs over the side of the bed. A nurse was called to help.

"What's he doing?" I asked.

His daughter smiled, tears of joy filling her eyes. "He wants to go to the window and wave goodbye to you."

When I walked to the elevator, he was standing and walking with the support of his daughter. In the parking lot, I glanced up to see her father—a new man—waving back at me from the third-floor window. What a joy to witness the miracle of his salvation and healing, but they hadn't needed me. Love nudged me to consider this man's heart language of Tagalog. Love urged me to include the young pastor. And love filled my heart with praise as I waved back.

LOVE IS . . .

If I could speak all the languages of earth and of angels, but didn't love others, I would only be a noisy gong or a clanging cymbal. If I had the gift of prophecy, and if I understood all of God's secret plans and possessed all knowledge, and if I had such faith that I could move mountains, but didn't love others, I would be nothing. If I gave everything I have to the poor and even sacrificed my body, I could boast about it; but if I didn't love others, I would have gained nothing.[4]

We can possess gifts of healing, speak in many different tongues, work miracles, speak prophecy, and so much more, but none of it matters, Paul says, if we don't love others. Jesus said, "Greater love has no one than this, that someone lay down his life for his friends."[5] The greatest love of all was revealed in Jesus when he laid down his life for us—while we were still sinners—and paid the price for our sins. Love is others focused. Love is sacrifice.

I will often hear believers say things like, "I'm called to this or that ministry," referencing how they serve in the church as their calling. This may be true, provided the Spirit has given you the spiritual gifts needed to operate in that calling. But more important than your calling, or your spiritual gifts, or your anointing, is your ability to love others like Jesus did. He is our example.

> Let each of you look not only to his own interests, but also to the interests of others. Have this mind among yourselves, which is yours in Christ Jesus, who, though he was in the form of God, did not count equality with God a thing to be grasped, but emptied himself, by taking the form of a servant, being born in the likeness of men. And being found in human form, he humbled himself by becoming obedient to the point of death, even death on a cross.[6]

Love does not think only of its own interests, but also of the interests of others. When we're working together as the body of Christ, we must choose love. Jesus was equal with the father, but he emptied himself and took the form of a servant, being born in human form. Love is willing, love is humble, love is obedient. These are not easy words, and I confess I often fail.

"Therefore be imitators of God," Paul wrote to the Ephesians, "as beloved children. And walk in love, as Christ loved us and gave himself up for us, a fragrant offering and sacrifice to God."[7] Jesus speaking to his disciples said, "A new commandment I give to you, that you love one another: just as I have loved you, you also are to love one another. By this all people will know that you are my disciples, if you have love for one another."[8]

REFLECTION & PRAYER

On one of our trips to Northern India in the foothills of the Himalayas, we stayed near Mussoorie where I noticed a man sitting in the same spot on the wall every day. He never spoke but sat looking over the plains below. After asking around, I discovered he came to that place every day and had been mute for several years. People who knew him said he was married and had two daughters, but had isolated himself from them. No one knew why. His name was Kumjram.

At that time and on those types of trips, I was often called upon to teach. But that morning, Kumjram caught my attention and I felt prompted by the Spirit to pray for him. No one else on our team seemed interested or willing, so I asked a local leader if he'd assist in translation. Several indigenous pastors and other missionaries joined us as we approached Kumjram and invited him to come join us in a nearby building for prayer. The building was often used as a chapel and seemed the best place to spend time in prayer with him.

"Holy Spirit," I began, "please show us how to pray for Kumjram." Then, without thinking much of it, I began to pray in tongues. The twelve or so others who were with us also began praying in tongues simultaneously, crying out to God for his healing. The cacophony of voices, all speaking in different languages, became more animated as the presence of God filled that place. It was incredible.

During our time of prayer together, it was revealed that what was needed was a deliverance prayer for the nine mute spirits that had taken up residence in Kumjram, resulting in years of silence and isolation. We began to call the demons out of him by the authority of Jesus, and one-by-one the evil spirits left. Kumjram's entire demeanor changed, and although he still had not spoken, we sensed that the demons had been cast out.

"Try to speak, Kumjram," someone in the group encouraged him. "Say the names of your two daughters."

He spoke after a long while, his voice reluctant and weak. We continued to encourage him, and eventually, he was able to say their names. We praised God and asked the Holy Spirit to seal the work that had taken place. I have not seen Kumjram since, but I've heard that after our visit, he began talking and engaging with his family and community.

I have seen many more people healed and delivered. I have seen the miracle of forgiveness and salvation. I have watched the Spirit move in ways I never could have imagined. How could I have known how the Spirit would use me at the church in Bulacan or in Kumjram's life? It's a good reminder to be available and open to the Holy Spirit who may choose to use you in ways you've never practiced, and also to be mindful of how the Spirit may want to use other believers in the room with you.

Love is the better way.

- Scriptures urge us to use our spiritual gifts, but also to choose love. How do you balance the tension between these two essentials? What stands out to you?
- In what ways do you feel you have failed to step out in your spiritual gifts? In what ways do you feel you have failed to love others when working within the body of Christ?
- Read Philippians 2:1–11 and Hebrews 12:1–17. In both passages, we are asked to consider Jesus. What do you notice about Jesus' motives and actions? How will you imitate him in these motives and actions?
- During Jesus' final days on earth, he began washing his disciples' feet. This is often referred to as servant leadership and is an excellent group activity. Find two friends and practice serving one another. While one person washes another's feet, the third person prays. Then switch until everyone has had their feet washed. What are your takeaways?

CHAPTER 11

POURING INTO OTHERS

O ur lives were changing. I'd become the Director of Ministries at our church and—together with Connie—was leading a small group through the Alpha course created by Nicky Gumbel. The course brought people together every week for a meal, fellowship, and a video teaching through God's Word. Connie was very involved with the meal preparations and would often make or purchase extra table decorations and supplies to make the meals as visually appealing as they were delicious.

At the time, we had a German exchange student staying with us. Week by week, Suzie saw the elaborate food preparations and eventually asked to join us. (I remember one week in particular where the fruit platter included a swan carved from an apple, with two slices of apple standing up as the wings.) We were delighted to have her join us and the group loved her. I noticed she was somewhat quiet during the discussion, so on the car ride home, as Suzie and Connie balanced dishes and leftover trays in their laps, I asked her what she thought about the evening.

"It wasn't really what I was expecting," she said slowly. She paused for a moment before adding, "I thought we would do more with . . . the food."

"The food?"

"Well, you know. I thought there would be more . . ." her voice trailed off and she motioned vaguely with her hands. Connie and I took turns guessing, but we had no idea what she was trying to communicate. We got along great with Suzie, but sometimes the language barrier really got in the way. After a few more guesses she finally said, "I thought there would be more preparing of the food."

By the time we pulled into our driveway, we realized Suzie thought Connie was teaching a weekly culinary or catering class. Surely, those incredible dishes had something to do with a cooking class! We all laughed and were relieved when Suzie confessed that she still enjoyed the group and would like to keep coming.

A few weeks later, the group went on a weekend retreat as part of the Alpha course. The teachings focused on the Holy Spirit: who he is, what he does, and how we can be filled with him. Suzie came with us and joined in the teachings and worship earnestly. Connie and I were thrilled to see her so eager as we'd tried to witness to her many times without much success. At the end of the weekend, Suzie surprised us all with a request to receive Jesus as her Lord and Savior and to be baptized in the Holy Spirit. She seemed to dance and float through the rest of the retreat, having encountered Jesus in a very real way.

Not long after, Suzie's parents arrived from Germany for a visit. Suzie had told them about her conversion experience, and although they were not Christians, they seemed comfortable with our beliefs and decided to leave Suzie with us for the remainder of her stay. Connie and I were thrilled. We had many more opportunities to help Suzie begin her new walk with the Lord, and formed a lasting friendship with her parents that would take a few twists and turns of its own.

SHARING OUR ABUNDANCE

I've had the privilege of serving with a number of different pastors and ministries. Each one drilled into me the importance of using my gifts, prayer, stepping out in faith, and relying on the Lord. But Dave Fischer of Gateway Church was especially instrumental in broadening my understanding of missions and pouring into others. My focus up to this point had been on ministering within the body of Christ to bring healing and wholeness to God's people in the US and abroad. Now I would be challenged to see an even bigger picture.

I had always been interested in missions work, but Dave helped me see the need to reach the lost, unreached people groups who had never had the opportunity to hear the name of Jesus or the good news of the gospel in their own language. I was reminded that Jesus had promised his return when every tribe, nation, and tongue had heard the good news. Dave was also kingdom minded. Whenever he was faced with a problem, he would always ask: What would be most beneficial in advancing God's kingdom? It was never about him or the popular vote, but what would be effective in winning souls for Christ.

I've found that every time I step out in faith to pour into others, the Spirit has met me and provided more abundantly than I thought possible. Simple encounters where I've followed the Spirit's leading have turned into lifelong friendships or opportunities to let the Spirit use me in someone's life. Pastors love to place all the importance on God's Word, referencing the prophet Isaiah.[1] And it's true. God's Word is important! But equally important is trusting the Spirit to lead us in our interactions and encounters, opening doors as only he can.

> For who knows a person's thoughts except the spirit of that person, which is in him? So also no one comprehends the thoughts of God except the Spirit of God. Now we have received not the spirit of the world, but the Spirit who is from God, that we might understand the things freely given us by God. And we impart this in words not taught by human

wisdom but taught by the Spirit, interpreting spiritual truths to those who are spiritual.[2]

In other words, if the Spirit knows the thoughts of God, and if we have received the Spirit, then we can understand the things that God is showing us and placing before us to do. In Galatians 5, Paul put it simply: "Since we are living by the Spirit, let us follow the Spirit's leading in every part of our lives."[3] When we are led by the Spirit, we can trust that God is at work in our daily interactions bringing about lasting, spiritual fruit.

Once, at a Wind of the Spirit Healing Conference in Baggio City, in the Philippines, twelve students showed up without having registered. They didn't have the funds, nor the essential materials to participate, but we couldn't just send them home; they'd walked three days to get there. The students were from a Bible school run by American missionaries, Delbert and Esther Rice, in Central Luzon.* Our team agreed to sponsor the students and provide the materials free of charge. It was a small thing to us, but we had no idea how far that gift would go.

After the conference, Wind of the Spirit decided to support one of the students, Matteo, through seminary. Years later, we supported him again in the construction of a new church building in the village of Beyonce, where he now serves as pastor. Our team traveled to his village and taught short seminars on the Holy Spirit in partnership with him several times. How incredible to watch Matteo mature from a young Bible college student into a man of God pastoring a church in his local village! I often think that the dividends we reaped in joy, partnering with him through prayer, far outweighed any financial gifts we gave him.

---

* Delbert and Esther had been running the Bible school there for many years. I visited them once, and as they were showing me through their house, I noticed they had a room dedicated to prayer. There was a single prayer rail along with a kneeling pad where they took their issues before the Lord. The kneeling pad was threadbare. I have no doubt their many prayers there played a significant role in our later connection with the Bible students.

Jay Jon was another student we developed a relationship with during this time. He lived in the Santa Fe region and was eager to develop a beekeeping program in his village to provide honey and pollination to the local farms. Our team supported this endeavor by providing consultation with a professional beekeeper in the States—Bob Martello. Bob was also one of our team members, and so, a few years later, we decided to visit Jay Jon to see how he was progressing.

The trip was more challenging than we anticipated. Upon our arrival in the Philippines, we discovered a local Islamic terrorist group had threatened abduction to anyone who came into Jay Jon's area. We were confident that the Holy Spirit was guiding us, so we went ahead with the trip anyway. From our base camp in Bayombong, we took a one-hour bus ride, then switched to a man-powered trike—the driver peddled in the front, while we sat on a small bench over the rear axles. He maneuvered us over dirt roads for about an hour before we finally transferred to motorcycles. At last, we found ourselves in a populated area with a few villages where someone was able to direct us to Jay Jon's home.

Jay Jon's home was crudely built; it was a small, modest wooden structure in the mountainous area of Nueva Vizcaya. He proudly introduced us to his mother before showing us around. The home was very dark and there wasn't much to see, but Jay Jon took great delight in having us there, and soon he began updating us on his beekeeping business.

"One of the big problems is theft," he said leading us toward the back of the house. "People steal the hives and drive off with them on their moto trikes. So, I had an idea." He grabbed a small ladder from the main living room and placed it against the back wall. "I keep the hive in my bedroom!"

Bob and I exchanged glances as Jay Jon scaled the ladder. Near the top, he pushed aside a small panel and climbed through. Then he motioned for us to follow. Once we were all inside, he replaced the panel and there was just enough room for us to stand up.

The attic space was very small. Near a tiny window covered with wire mesh was the hive. The bees flew freely in and out of the window, back and forth to their hive, while larger bugs and animals were kept out. With the panel in place, a small bed could be rolled out into the center of the room on which to sleep. Jay Jon's solution was ingenious, but also very difficult—not to mention, uncomfortable. Jay Jon didn't seem to mind. Bob and I prayed for him and his mother before heading back to our base camp, where we both reflected on his joy in spite of the challenges, and the stark contrast between our living conditions in the States and his.

The next morning, we were surprised to see Jay Jon walk into our seminar meeting. He approached us and held out a white plastic bag.

"You came to my house, and I didn't even offer you a drink of water," he said. "I'm so sorry. Please accept these vegetables from my garden as appreciation for your visit."

Bob and I had made the arduous journey to and from his village the day prior on buses, trikes, and motorcycles, but Jay Jon didn't have the resources for that. He must have walked most of the night to be able to be with us so early in the morning! We hugged and cried, and prayed with him again before he left. His generosity amazed me. He had so little, and yet he had given so much. This was a lesson I would not soon forget.

—————

Ricardo was another one of the students that Wind of the Spirit had supported and who we remained in contact with. After our initial meeting, Connie and I decided to pay for his seminary training, books, and accommodations. After praying about his situation, we realized that the cost to pay for everything was the equivalent of about one latte a day in the States. We could hardly believe it—for such a small sacrifice, we could change someone's entire future! We had no idea how the Lord might use this offering, but over the years we had the joy of watching him graduate seminary and marry his wife, Agnes. We even participated in their wedding through our donation of a pig for their two families to roast during their weeks-long celebration.

I've since had several opportunities to visit Ricardo and Agnes. As the pastor in a small rural village, Ricardo lives on community land and receives a very small income. He grows food on the land to provide for his family (which now includes three children), and shares much of the produce with his congregation and community. On one of those visits, I told Ricardo how proud Connie and I were of him, and how pleased we'd been to support him in seminary.

"Not just me!" he protested. "I shared the support you gave with five other students less fortunate than me." I could hardly believe it. He'd shared the gift he received with others.

"It's our culture," he explained. "When one has an abundance, you share it with those who have little."

SOWING TO THE KINGDOM

There are promises throughout Scripture about giving and generosity. But in Matthew 25, Jesus gives his followers a new understanding of generosity and hospitality.

> For I was hungry and you gave me food, I was thirsty and you gave me drink, I was a stranger and you welcomed me, I was naked and you clothed me, I was sick and you visited me, I was in prison and you came to me.[4]

His followers were understandably confused. *When did we do that for you, Lord?* They asked. *When did we see you hungry. When were you in prison, or a stranger, and sick?*

> And the King will answer them, "Truly, I say to you, as you did it to one of the least of these my brothers, you did it to me."

Then he will say to those on his left, "Depart from me, you cursed, into the eternal fire prepared for the devil and his angels. For I was hungry and you gave me no food, I was thirsty and you gave me no drink, I was a stranger and you did not welcome me, naked and you did not clothe me, sick and in prison and you did not visit me."[5]

When we live in the Spirit and are led by the Spirit, our generosity—whether that be a word of encouragement from God's Word or a financial gift—is sown into the kingdom of heaven. It is God who supplies the seeds and God who provides the increase. But only by walking in step with the Spirit will we know where and how to participate in the work he is doing. And it is only by giving yourself away and sharing what you have with others—your time, your resources, your finances, and your home—that you get to see the work he is doing.

He who supplies seed to the sower and bread for food will supply and multiply your seed for sowing and increase the harvest of your righteousness. You will be enriched in every way to be generous in every way, which through us will produce thanksgiving to God. For the ministry of this service is not only supplying the needs of the saints but is also overflowing in many thanksgivings to God.[6]

DIVINE OPPORTUNITIES

Our friendship with our German exchange student Suzie and her parents continued for many years. About a year after Suzie left, we traveled to Dresden to visit her family and then visited again a few years after that. It was on this trip that I realized I still carried some resentment toward the German people for the Second World War and the death of my father. I imagine Suzie's father Deiter had similar resentments; the Allies had bombed and destroyed sections of Dresden—his hometown.

After a few translated conversations with him about the devastation in Dresden and the past, I finally asked Suzie to tell him that we didn't need to carry things forward from the previous generation. We were both just little boys at the time. Although nothing more was said, I sensed I needed to say this for myself as much as for Deiter. Sometimes the Holy Spirit reveals little ways we're still holding onto hurts, unforgiveness, and issues from the past. We need to forgive and let go in preparation for what he's going to do next.

A few years later, our family made another trip to Dresden, but this time, I wanted to visit a small church near Suzie's family home in the village of Herrnhut. I'd just completed a fifteen-week comprehensive study on missions, called Perspectives on the World Christian Movement, where I learned about the Moravian missionaries who went out from this church in East Germany.* They'd had a huge impact on global missions, and I was eager to see the church in person. After some explanation, Suzie's mom seemed interested and even invited a few of her friends to join us. (By this time, Suzie's parents had split up, but we maintained a relationship with each of them.)

The museum was closing when our small group arrived, but they agreed to let us take a tour. Susie and her mother's friend Klaus, an elderly professor of microbiology, were the only Germans who spoke English and interpreted for us. The Moravian church in Herrnhut sent their first missionaries out in the 1730s and eventually had three hundred missionaries all over the world. They began a 24/7 continuous prayer watch that lasted for over a hundred years.

As Klaus read and translated the various graphics and texts on John Wesley and Count Zinzendorf's discussions on the Holy Spirit, he began to tear up. Prior to the war, Klaus had been raised in a Lutheran church. The oppressive post-war East German government reminded him of the persecution the Moravians experienced in Czechoslovakia, except the Moravians had found refuge on Count Zinzendorf's land

---

* The class had been introduced at Gateway Church by Dave Fischer, who'd challenged and influenced my understanding of global missions.

where the church now sits. Zinzendorf's work to bring unity and brotherly love led to a revival, and later, the Moravian's global missions and prayer work.

Years later, the young missionary John Wesley encountered some of those Moravian missionaries on a ship headed for the colony of Georgia. When a violent storm hit, they were in danger of being shipwrecked. While John and everyone else panicked, he caught sight of the Moravian missionaries praying and singing. They were full of peace and, he realized, they had something he didn't. He was encouraged by their presence.

After wrestling with this for several years, Wesley traveled back to England where, at a chapel meeting in Aldersgate, he read Martin Luther's preface to the book of Romans and received the Holy Spirit. He would later write that the moment he received the Spirit, his heart was "strangely warmed."

When Klaus began to open up and share stories of his childhood church and faith, we knew we were standing in the midst of a holy moment. Klaus had only come because we invited Suzie's mother; we'd only met Suzie's mother because of Suzie's encounter with the Holy Spirit through the Alpha course; we met Suzie because we'd been open to having a German exchange student stay with us; and we'd only come to Herrnhut because I recently completed the Perspectives course where I learned about the Moravian missionaries.

REFLECTION & PRAYER

It always amazes me how the Holy Spirit weaves our lives together—events, people, and experiences. We are participants in what the Spirit is doing even though we don't see the whole picture. He is always working, even when we don't understand what he's doing. I needed to have that moment of letting go and forgiving the German people with Deiter, who I suspect needed it too. It opened me up to share in the work the Holy Spirit was doing that day in Klaus. What might seem random to us is often part of a much larger plan in which Jesus is glorified in ways we never could have imagined.

- Describe a time when you saw the Holy Spirit work and move through people or events outside of yourself, or a time when you saw him divinely thread together what you thought were unrelated events. What did you think of those individual moments when they happened? Did they feel holy? How do you feel about those moments now that the Holy Spirit has revealed they are strung together? What are your takeaways?

- Have you partnered with missionaries or nationals who are doing the Lord's work? I encourage you to reach out to them and connect with them on a personal level. Ask your church for their list of missionaries and start praying for them and emailing them. Expanding our understanding of God's kingdom and pouring into others is a wonderful way to see the Holy Spirit work.

- John Wesley realized that the Moravian missionaries had something he didn't have. He was a believer, but the power of the Holy Spirit had not yet been manifested in his life. This is true for many Christians, I think. Do you have a holy desire for something more in the Spirit? Trust that he has divinely orchestrated this moment for you, then ask him, "Spirit, show me how to go deeper with you. What am I missing?"

CHAPTER 12

NEW SEASONS WITH THE HOLY SPIRIT

"I see a white signpost at a crossroad junction, pointing in all different directions. But one of the arrows is pointing toward Galbraith," I said.

I'd never heard of a place called Galbraith, but by now I'd developed a habit of sharing whatever came into my mind during prayer. It was usually the Holy Spirit. What meant absolutely nothing to me often held great significance for either the person we were praying for, or someone else on the team.

Pastor Larry and I were in a small town in the Midwest for a Wind of the Spirit Ministry weekend at a local church. We hadn't been there long when the pastor invited us to join him on his ministry rounds. One of his parishioners was in a nursing home and had requested prayer. As we stood praying around his bedside, I saw the image of the crossroad.

The pastor seemed surprised. "I know a man named Galbraith," he said. "He's in a care home across town. Maybe we should go visit him and see how he's doing."

Across town, we found Galbraith in a double-occupancy room. He was not well and appeared to be nearing the end of his life. We began praying for the comfort and healing of God to fill his body, but nothing more was revealed. *Perhaps the Holy Spirit had sent us here simply to pray with and comfort Galbraith?* We said our goodbyes and got up to leave.

"Wait," the man in the next bed said softly. "Before you go, would you please pray for me too?"

Of course, we gladly prayed for him, but I sensed from the Holy Spirit through prayer that he was not yet saved. When we finished praying, I quietly mentioned it to the others.

Pastor Larry turned to the man and asked him directly, "Have you ever accepted Jesus as your Lord and Savior?"

"No," he said.

"I think we should do that now. Would you like to?" The man nodded his head and Pastor Larry led him into the saving grace of Jesus Christ.

I often reflect on this experience, and the image of the crossroads and signpost. It meant nothing to me, but it had great significance in ways I couldn't have comprehended without sharing it with the group. The Lord was leading us to Galbraith and another one of his lost sheep. It's a good reminder that what may seem insignificant or nonsensical to us, just might be the Holy Spirit directing our steps. But we must be willing to obey: share the vision, take a step of faith, pray out loud and with other believers, and risk looking foolish.

This experience, and others like it, became one of the foundation stones in my faith-walk with the Holy Spirit. I could trust him even when the request seemed strange or the situation uncertain. Through years of talking with him, following him, and listening to him, I have learned the sound of his voice and am willing to obey.

SEASONS OF CHANGE

Connie and I have had many different seasons walking with the Lord. Our early years as believers were spent at Silverdale United Methodist Church. After about twenty-five years, the Lord moved us on to Hillcrest Assemblies of God in Bremerton, under the leadership of Pastor Scott Fontenot who was a former missionary in Southeast Asia.

One of my favorite things to do was to go to church early on weekday mornings to pray in tongues with Pastor Scott and other church leaders. Pastor Scott told me on numerous occasions how much he valued our time together in prayer. He likened it to the offensive line in American football—their primary job is to create openings for the running backs to break through the opposition and score, or at least advance their ground.

"That's what happens during our times of prayer," he once told me. "When you and the leaders are praying, I feel like I'm gaining more access and revelation as to what God wants to say and do in our church!" I was greatly encouraged by this thought and considered it a privilege to pray with him. He encouraged me to use my gifts, and allowed me to teach classes on the Holy Spirit.* But it was his love of missions that would have the greatest impact on my life.

Around that time, Hillcrest joined a coalition of local churches with the purpose of bringing the gospel to the unreached people of Garhwal, in the foothills of the Himalayas in Northern India. The group was formed by the pastor of Gateway Church, Mark Paterson, and became known as the Garhwal Alliance. Sadly, Pastor Mark was later diagnosed with Lou Gehrig's disease. He continued to lead both Gateway Church and the Alliance, but his health quickly declined.

Pastor Scott had hoped to spend more time with Pastor Mark with the desire to write his biography, but tragically, this never happened. Pastor Scott developed a serious brain tumor that required surgery. During this time, he asked if I would attend the Garhwal Alliance meetings on behalf of our church. I loved representing Hillcrest at these meetings and enjoyed spending time with the missionaries from India and other pastors who shared their love for missions. It was at these meetings that I met Dave Fischer who, as I mentioned previously, had a significant impact on my life in the years ahead.

Pastor Scott was eventually scheduled for surgery to remove the tumor, however, during the procedure, he suffered a stroke. Due to the

---

* SHAPE for Ministry was a program designed by Saddleback Church in Irvine, CA.

nature of his surgery, the stroke went largely undetected and consequently resulted in more serious physical complications from which he would never fully recover. It was especially difficult to watch my pastor —the man who had encouraged me spiritually and opened my eyes to missions—fight without much success.

I continued to represent Hillcrest at the Garhwal Alliance meetings, but I was torn. My heart was with Pastor Scott in his valiant struggle, but I also very clearly felt the Holy Spirit redirecting us. Although it was a difficult decision, I wanted to follow where the Lord was leading, and Connie agreed. We joined Gateway Church, having already connected with them through the Garhwal Alliance.

SEASONS OF LOSS & NEW BEGINNINGS

During this time of transition, Connie and I decided to take a trip, driving through the southern states to visit friends who lived there. We'd grown tired of the long, gray, wet winters of the Pacific Northwest and wondered if perhaps the Lord might move us somewhere else for the winter. On a visit with our friend (and my Wind of the Spirit prayer partner) Anne Key, we fell in love with Fernandina Beach on Amelia Island in Florida. We loved its small-town feel, its rich history, and the sense of community. And we loved being close to our friend Anne.

Anne and I dreamed of starting a healing ministry similar to Wind of the Spirit, so we prayed and invited Pastors Larry and Audrey to visit us with that in mind. Sometime later, I made a second trip to Fernandina; this time I was guided by the Holy Spirit to buy a small house in the historic district. It was a very old building and in need of a lot of work—just the sort of thing I loved to do—and was listed at a price we could afford without selling our home in Silverdale. I emailed the photos to Connie and she agreed. We signed the contract and began a new season together.

As soon as we arrived in Fernandina, Connie, Anne, and I began talking with local pastors about our vision to start a healing ministry. Meanwhile, I worked on the house while Connie furnished it with purchases from garage sales and local antique stores. Anne introduced us to her church, Living Waters. We loved the pastor, the people, and their style of worship. We joined Anne's home fellowship group during a study on the Jewish Roots of Christianity, where we learned about the various Jewish festivals and how they tied into the Scriptures and the story of Jesus. I also attended another Bible study similar to Bible Study Fellowship, and we quickly began to feel at home in Fernandina.

Anne had been regularly taking us on trips to get to know the area and learn more about the local history. On one particular day, we planned to visit Okefenokee, the famous swamp, but Anne never showed. We phoned her at home—no reply. After about an hour, we drove to her house, but although her car was in the driveway, no one answered the door. At this point, we were very concerned. Connie found Anne's hidden key and walked upstairs to find Anne on the landing between her bedroom and the bathroom. She'd had a stroke and couldn't move or speak. We called emergency services, and she was immediately taken to the hospital in Jacksonville, about thirty miles away.

For the next few months, we spent many hours with Anne at different hospitals and clinics—she became the focus of our lives that winter. Although we had no hand in her healing, our finding her when we did most likely saved her life. *Was this the reason the Holy Spirit had directed us to Fernandina?* Anne survived the stroke, but despite her efforts in physical therapy, her mind and body never recovered to the level we all hoped.

As spring rolled around, Connie and I made plans to return to Silverdale. While we were praying about what to do with our Fernandina house for the summer, the Holy Spirit reminded us of a single mother at our church, Angie, and her daughter Isabella. We'd met them at our church, Living Waters. We offered them the house rent free for the summer. Angie was incredibly thankful; it was an opportunity for her to pay off some debt and save toward their future. We said our goodbyes, but our friendship with Angie and connection with Living Waters Church continued.

Connie and I continued to travel to Fernandina over the winter for several years. During that time, Angie announced her engagement to Mike (a man I met at the men's Bible study) and requested marriage counseling from Connie and me. We loved getting to be a part of their lives, but after a while the travel began to wear on us. We both grew tired of the disruption, and never really felt at home in either location. We made a plan to travel back to Fernandina one more time in the next few weeks. But before we even left Silverdale, we received a phone call from a neighbor in Fernandina.

"I just met an older couple that really likes your house. Would it be all right if I show them around inside?"

With our blessing, our neighbor Vickie showed them around. The next day the couple called us.

"We love your home. Please let us know if you ever decide to sell it. We would love to buy it."

Even though the house wasn't on the market, we agreed to sell it to them. They wanted to pay in cash and agreed to our price. We planned to meet in Fernandina the following week; they wired me the earnest money that evening. Not long after, Connie and I flew down to Fernandina to visit with friends and help with Angie and Mike's wedding preparations. We were thrilled to be a part of their wedding and delighted to celebrate with them, marking the end of a very interesting chapter in our lives.

Seasons of Letting Go

During one of our back-and-forth trips from Fernandina to Silverdale, I attended a meeting at the Silverdale United Methodist Church. Although Connie and I no longer attended the church, it always felt like home as it was the place where I came to the Lord and received the Holy Spirit. Still, our departure from the church had come as the result of a disagreement, and although I'd forgiven those involved, there was still someone there I did not want to run into.

I parked my car and walked through the door leading to the church offices at the very moment the person I did not want to see was leaving. We practically bumped into each other. We both paused, unsure of what to do, and stood face-to-face for what seemed like ages. Finally, we moved toward each other in the way of an awkward greeting. It was not a warm hug, but I realized in hindsight that the Holy Spirit had orchestrated what I had tried to avoid. I had forgiven this person, yes, but there was still more forgiveness, letting go, and reconciliation needed.

Not long after, my very good friend and Christian brother, Dick Cooke passed away. Dick had been a mentor of mine and was a leader at Bible Study Fellowship. His memorial was to be held at the church of a man who'd been part of a church split years earlier; a split in which I had no part, but had been personally hurt by his actions and attempts to involve me. Again, I had forgiven the man (or so I thought), but I did not want to see him. My allegiance to my friend Dick won out, and I attended the memorial.

I planned to arrive at the last minute so as to not run into anyone before the service. I pulled into one of the few remaining spots as far away from the church building as possible and began making my way across the crowded parking lot. It was then that I realized I had inadvertently parked next to the church offices, and the pastor I did not want to see was making a last-minute dash in my direction to grab some forgotten item for the memorial.

We greeted each other with a clumsy exchange of words and formalities.

"Hello Mr. Cashmore."

"Hello Pastor."

After another awkward pause, we extended our arms in a half-hearted hug. I think it's safe to say we were both surprised. Nothing more was said, but after he delivered an encouraging and hopeful message in celebration of Dick's life, I realized I couldn't let that season of hurt continue any longer. So often in life, we think our hearts are clean; that we've forgiven or let go. But our attitudes reveal something else entirely. We need to let the Spirit guide us, rather than doing what our flesh tells us to do. The situations he leads us into aren't always fun, but they are necessary.

SEASONS OF LONELINESS

Back in Bremerton, Connie and I became more involved with Gateway Church. I joined the Men's Round Table, a discipleship group that meets every Saturday morning to sharpen one another and stay on course in our relationships with the Lord. The men are from different churches around the Poulsbo area, but in spite of our differences, it has become a safe place for men to learn and grow together. Proverbs 27:17 says, "Iron sharpens iron, and one man sharpens another." I've seen many men receive the baptism of the Holy Spirit there, and many more delivered from ungodly soul-ties and unforgiveness.

I first realized the importance and power of small groups, and particularly men's and women's groups, years earlier while I was still at Silverdale United Methodist Church. I'd noticed two men there who talked often and seemed to enjoy a close friendship. I had some male acquaintances, but none of them were close or in my same season of life. Watching their friendship made me realize I was lonely.

"I really admire your friendship with Terry," I said to Dennis one Sunday. I felt a bit awkward approaching him, but I felt convicted by the Holy Spirit to do something about my loneliness ever since I became aware of it. "Would you be open to becoming friends with me as well?"

Dennis, Terry, and I later met for coffee where we discussed how lonely American men are, and how our independence is hurting our spiritual growth as Christian men.

Not long after, we began inviting other men who we guessed felt the same way we did. This group eventually became a large group that met at my home weekly. The Promise Keepers movement was just beginning to emerge in the Pacific Northwest, and we soon allied ourselves with their organization. More and more men wanted to be a part of our home group. Dennis and a few other men led worship, we had a time of studying the Word, and made ourselves accountable to one another in our walk with Jesus. Friendships grew, men were baptized with the Holy Spirit, and God moved.

After about twelve years, the group had become so big that the intimacy of our earlier small group was lost. We split our large group into four smaller groups that met in various parts of the county. Once a month we all met together. For a while it was productive, but slowly the groups began to fizzle out as relationships were stretched and less people were attending. It was never quite the same as when we first began meeting. Still, friendships were established that continue to this day, and we know God has a purpose in everything.

REFLECTION & PRAYER

We like to think that in every difficulty we can find a lesson, and in every season there will be closure or understanding. *Oh, I know what that was about. Yes, I see what the Holy Spirit was doing in my life there.* But that just isn't the case. "For now we see in a mirror dimly," Paul wrote in 1 Corinthians 13:12, "but then face to face. Now I know in part; then I shall know fully, even as I have been fully known."

One day we will see clearly. One day we will understand. But until then, we walk by faith. We trust God. We learn to listen to the voice of his Spirit speaking to us, guiding us, directing us, and we practice following him. We obey.

> For my thoughts are not your thoughts, neither are your ways my ways, declares the LORD. For as the heavens are higher than the earth, so are my ways higher than your ways and my thoughts than your thoughts. "For as the rain and the snow come down from heaven and do not return there but water the earth, making it bring forth and sprout, giving seed to the sower and bread to the eater, so shall my word be that goes out from my mouth; it shall not return to me empty, but it shall accomplish that which I purpose, and shall succeed in the thing for which I sent it.[1]

- Reflect on a season in your life or ministry where you clearly felt the Spirit leading you, but were left with uncertainty. Perhaps it didn't end well or didn't follow the trajectory you hoped it would. Talk to the Holy Spirit about what you wanted or expected to happen. Ask the Spirit to talk to you about the situation. How does he see it? Is there anything he'd like you to know about it?
- Do you have close spiritual friendships? Safe people with whom you can be honest and be held accountable? Is there anyone in your community who may need a close spiritual friendship or mentor like you? Ask the Holy Spirit about them. Follow his lead.
- Read 1 Corinthians 13:12 and consider: What does it mean to see "in a mirror dimly"? How might you apply this to the season you're in or seasons you've already experienced?
- Can you think of an area in your life where you are losing heart? Ask the Holy Spirit to show you how to think about the things that are concerning you. Ask him to show you how to pray and to direct your steps.

EPILOGUE

I've lived a wonderful, wonderful life. Connie and I have now been married for forty years, and I recently celebrated my eighty-fourth birthday. We still live in the beach cabin God gave us on Dyes Inlet. We have three wonderful children, six grandkids, and two great-grandkids. We continue to serve in our church and regularly host times of fellowship in our home.

It has been incredible to reminisce about all that God has done over the years; how the Spirit has led both me and Connie, and how he's used us. But as much as I've enjoyed looking back and praising God for what he's done, I'm reminded that the story continues. What began as an incredible adventure with the Holy Spirit all those years ago has not faded with age or time. Even at my age, the Spirit is still using me and I know he will continue to do so until the day he calls me home.

I wanted to write this book as a legacy for my children, but as I began writing, I realized that the stories I really wanted to tell weren't just of where I was born or how I came to the States. I wanted to tell the story of how Jesus saved me, how the Spirit has led me, and how God has used me over the years; the manifestations of the Spirit that I've been privileged to witness; the healing, restoration, and wholeness I've found;

and the freedom others have found through forgiveness. I wanted to tell the best story I know—the story of God's great love for you and for me.

In 1 Samuel 16, the prophet Samuel anoints the young shepherd boy David with oil in recognition of his calling as the future king of Israel. In the Old Testament, both people and tools were anointed with oil. Although we often use the term *anointed* to mean *special ability*, it really means "consecrated" or "set apart for sacred use." Jesus was anointed with oil in Bethany, and also anointed with water and the Spirit during his baptism. And, as we've discussed in earlier chapters, Jesus has anointed you—the Church—with the oil of his Holy Spirit. It is a necessary component and a commissioning for the calling he has placed upon your life.

I hope that in reading my story, you will be encouraged to go on your own adventure with the Holy Spirit. I hope you will be inspired to go deeper with Jesus than you ever have before. And I hope you will take my story even further as you fulfill your own calling, anointed by the Spirit, to spread his good news wherever you go.

> And Jesus came and said to them, "All authority in heaven and on earth has been given to me. Go therefore and make disciples of all nations, baptizing them in the name of the Father and of the Son and of the Holy Spirit, teaching them to observe all that I have commanded you. And behold, I am with you always, to the end of the age."[1]

NOTES

INTRODUCTION

1. 2 Corinthians 5:17
2. Ephesians 5:18, NLT
3. Acts 2:14–21
4. Acts 19:1–6, NLT
5. John 14:16, AMP

1. THE HELPER

1. Acts 2:1–4, NIV
2. Acts 2:14–18, NIV
3. See Acts 1:8, John 16:12-15, John 14:15–18
4. Genesis 1:1-2
5. Matthew 28:19
6. 2 Corinthians 13:14, NLT
7. Romans 8:11
8. Ephesians 3:16–19, NIV
9. Acts 8:18
10. 1 Timothy 4:14
11. Hebrews 6:1, 2
12. Acts 8:17
13. Luke 11:9–13, NIV

2. LEARNING TO SPEAK

1. Acts 2:5–8, NIV
2. Acts 10:44–46, NIV
3. Acts 19:4–6, NIV
4. Matthew 3:1–2
5. Matthew 11:9–10, NIV
6. John 14:6
7. John 14:16–18, NIV
8. John 3:3
9. John 3:5–6, NIV
10. Romans 5:12, 15, NIV
11. 1 Peter 2:2, NIV
12. 1 Corinthians 13:11, NIV
13. 1 Corinthians 3:1–2, NIV
14. Jude 20, NIV

15. Ephesians 6:18
16. 1 Corinthians 14:15–17, NIV
17. Romans 7:15, NIV
18. John 4:4–9, NIV
19. John 4:10–14, NIV

3. Learning to Listen

1. Acts 13:2, NIV
2. Acts 20:22–23, NIV
3. See 1 Samuel 3:4–7
4. 1 Samuel 3:4–10, NIV
5. 1 Kings 19:11–13, NIV
6. John 10:27
7. Hebrews 3:15

4. Spiritual Warfare

1. Luke 3:22
2. Luke 4:1–2
3. Luke 4:1–4
4. Luke 4:5–8
5. Luke 4:9–12
6. 1 Peter 5:6–9
7. James 4:7
8. Ephesians 6:12
9. Ephesians 6:13–18
10. Philippians 4:6–7
11. Luke 10:20
12. 1 John 4:4
13. Romans 8:26–27

5. Following the Spirit's Lead

1. John 6:6
2. Acts 8:28, NIV
3. Acts 8:29, NIV
4. Malachi 3:7b–10
5. Malachi 3:10b
6. Luke 21:1–4, NLT
7. Romans 8:14–15
8. Luke 6:38
9. Matthew 22:21, NLT

6. Forgiveness

1. Matthew 18:32–33, NLT
2. Matthew 18:35, NLT
3. Matthew 6:14–15
4. 1 John 1:9
5. Psalm 103:12
6. Matthew 5:20
7. Matthew 5:21–22
8. Galatians 3:19, NLT
9. Galatians 3:2–3
10. Hebrews 12:15
11. Jeremiah 17:9
12. 2 Corinthians 4:7, NLT

7. Healing & Restoration

1. Mark 1:40–42
2. Mark 1:45
3. 2 Corinthians 5:18–19
4. 2 Corinthians 5:20
5. John 7:37–38
6. John 4:13–14
7. Romans 5:5
8. Number 20:8

8. Bearing Spiritual Fruit

1. Galatians 2:20
2. 2 Timothy 3:5
3. Matthew 7:16–17
4. Titus 3:5, NIV
5. John 15:5

9. Praying in the Spirit

1. 1 Corinthians 12:8–11
2. Romans 12:6–9
3. Ephesians 4:16, NLT

10. Working Together

1. 1 Corinthians 12:28
2. 1 Corinthians 12:31a, NLT
3. 1 Corinthians 12:31b, NLT

4. 1 Corinthians 13:1–3, NLT
5. John 15:13
6. Philippians 2:4–8
7. Ephesians 5:1–2
8. John 13:34–35

11. POURING INTO OTHERS

1. Isaiah 55:11
2. 1 Corinthians 2:11–13
3. Galatians 5:25, NLT
4. Matthew 25:35–36
5. Matthew 25:40–43
6. 2 Corinthians 9:10–12

12. NEW SEASONS WITH THE HOLY SPIRIT

1. Isaiah 55:8–11

EPILOGUE

1. Matthew 28:18–20

About the Author

Born and raised in England, **Bob Cashmore** spent the first half of his life doing things his own way—often making a mess of it. After moving to the United States in search of a fresh start, he continued to stumble until 1984, when he surrendered his life to Jesus Christ. Filled with the Holy Spirit soon after, Bob began a lifelong journey of transformation marked by grace, purpose, and hope.

Together with his wife of forty years, Connie, Bob has served the Lord through teaching, prayer, and ministry both at home and abroad. His ministry has included years of service with Wind of the Spirit Ministries, multiple mission trips to the Philippines, India, North Africa, and Senegal, and leadership roles in several churches, including Silverdale United Methodist Church, Hillcrest Assembly, and Gateway Fellowship in Poulsbo, Washington.

Bob's greatest joy has been witnessing the Holy Spirit move—in healing, in forgiveness, and in the lives changed by God's power. His desire is to encourage others to walk closely with the Spirit, to trust His leading, and to experience the same transforming love that changed his life all those years ago.

He and Connie live in Washington State, where they continue to serve their church community and host times of prayer and fellowship in their home. Today, Bob continues to teach and minister through prayer, guided by the leading of the Holy Spirit.

ACKNOWLEDGMENTS

There have been so many people who have welcomed me, shared Christ with me, encouraged me, given me opportunities to teach, and shown me Jesus through their lives. Some planted seeds, others watered, and still others were part of the harvest. You have all made a difference, and I thank God for each of you.

To Sam Johnston and the Boys' Brigade Officers, who planted the first seeds of faith in my heart as a teenager.

To Jack and Ruby Langill, my spiritual parents, who watered and nurtured those seeds thirty years later as they faithfully discipled me through the years.

To the Body of Christ at Silverdale United Methodist Church, who welcomed me into their fellowship, nurtured me in the faith, and entrusted me with leadership.

To Pastors Larry and Audry Eddings, for bringing healing and wholeness to my life through Wind of the Spirit Ministries, and for allowing me to grow as part of the teaching team—ministering to others in the power of the Holy Spirit.

To Dick Cooke and the other teaching leaders at Bible Study Fellowship, whose faithful teaching helped me go deeper into God's Word for so many years.

To Doug Weeks, for his friendship as a new believer and for introducing me to the Walk to Emmaus movement, where I learned foundational truths about walking with Jesus.

To Dave Fischer, for his encouragement and leadership on short-term mission trips to India, North Africa, and Senegal, West Africa.

To Dennis Rickabaugh, my faithful friend and companion in men's ministry for more than fifteen years—thank you for always being there, Dennis.

To Bob Wrenn, for your encouragement, home fellowship, and friendship during our winters in Florida, and for sharing in worship at Living Waters.

To Mary Pero, for your prayers, wisdom, and support in shaping this book into more than I ever imagined it could be.

And to my dear wife, Connie—thank you for your love and steadfast support through forty years of marriage. Thank you for trusting me with your heart.

Finally, to the hundreds of brothers and sisters in Christ whom I have not named here but who have influenced my life and allowed me to share in their walk with Jesus—thank you.

www.ingramcontent.com/pod-product-compliance
Lightning Source LLC
La Vergne TN
LVHW021346080426
835508LV00020B/2132